PETE
EYEWITNESS
of His
MAJESTY

PETER: EYEWITNESS of His MAJESTY

as Disciple, Preacher, Pastor

Edward Donnelly

THE BANNER OF TRUTH TRUST

THE BANNER OF TRUTH TRUST
3 Murrayfield Road, Edinburgh EH12 6EL
P.O.Box 621, Carlisle, Pennsylvania 17013, USA

*

© Edward Donnelly 1998
First published 1998
ISBN 0 85151 744 7

*

*

Typeset in 11/12 pt New Baskerville by
Hewer Text Limited, Edinburgh
Printed in Finland by WSOY

To Lorna

ACKNOWLEDGEMENTS

This book began life as messages preached at two pastors' conferences: in Bala, North Wales, under the auspices of the Evangelical Movement of Wales, and in Trinity Baptist Church, Montville, New Jersey. I would like to thank my brother ministers who so graciously received the addresses on those occasions and who enriched my understanding in subsequent discussion.

Thanks are due also to Al Martin for his helpful comments on an early draft of the manuscript and for all that his friendship means to me; and to my editor, Hywel Jones, who is responsible for many of the virtues and none of the faults of the following pages and who strikes a perfect balance, for this writer, of gentle pressure and unremitting encouragement.

My deepest earthly gratitude is to my family: for the memory of my late father, Edward, and to my mother, Isobel, inseparable in my mind and both reminding me in different ways of Peter at his best; to loving and supportive children, Catherine, Ruth and John; most of all, to Lorna, all that a wife could ever be.

CONTENTS

1

Introducing Peter

The Apostle Peter has been undervalued for too long. In some respects he is the best known of the disciples of Jesus. His name has been borrowed for baby boys and church buildings in every continent and throughout history. Most people, even those with a minimal knowledge of the New Testament, could identify him as one of the Twelve. They may not be able to name all the other disciples, but they are familiar with Peter.

Yet, in another sense, he is scarcely known at all. The Peter of popular imagination is a blurred figure, more mythical than real. His image has been shaped by best-selling novels such as *The Big Fisherman* or the earlier *Quo Vadis?*, for which the author received a Nobel Prize. These books were later turned into films and have influenced millions. But they are works of fiction, owing as much to legend and imagination as to history, and they can teach us nothing worthwhile about the apostle. The common idea of Saint Peter sitting at the pearly gates with his bunch of keys is based on a misunderstanding of Christ's promise in Matthew 16:19: 'I will give you the keys of the kingdom of heaven'. In these mists of fantasy the real man is in danger of being lost.

Evangelicals too have tended to neglect Peter. Perhaps this has been a reaction against the extravagant claims of Roman Catholicism, which teaches that he was the earthly head of the church, the predecessor of all succeeding bishops of Rome and the source of their authority. Such assertions have no basis either in the New Testament or in history and would have grieved the humble heart of a man who described himself as 'a fellow elder' (*1 Pet.* 5:1). But this exaltation of Peter for reasons of church politics may well have frightened Protestants into giving him less attention than he deserves.

We identify more closely with Paul. His dramatic conversion has served as the pattern for many a subsequent 'Damascus road' experience. His brilliant exposition of such doctrines as justification through faith alone speaks to the heart of our Reformation theology and life. We have concentrated on the Pauline epistles and are familiar with the various emphases of his teaching. By contrast, Peter seems a rather one-dimensional figure, lovable and accessible in the ups and downs of his discipleship, but lacking in depth and interest. In comparison with Paul, he has been the subject of little serious study.[1]

But this is unfair to a major New Testament personality. A large amount of material in the Gospels is devoted to him and he is named first in all their lists of the disciples. He is the chief figure in the first part of Acts and, as Scripture draws to a close, is the author of two epistles.[2] Peter's character is vivid, complex and well-rounded. His leadership was decisive in the history of the church. His teaching is profound and compellingly up-to-date. It is time that he was better known.

This book is no more than a beginning, in which I would like to introduce you to a man whom I have come to respect and love. It is not a biography of Peter, not a study of his theology nor an exposition of his letters. It is simply a brief look at him from three angles. In the Gospels we will see him as a disciple, discovering steadily — sometimes painfully — what it means to follow Jesus. We will then listen to him as an apostle, preaching powerfully in the early chapters of Acts,

---

[1] Chief among notable exceptions to this neglect are Hugh Martin's *Simon Peter* (repr. Banner of Truth Trust, 1984) which is a profound and eloquent analysis of 'the great leading principles of the divine life common to Peter and all Christian men' (p. 5) and J. Glyn Owen's *From Simon to Peter* (Welwyn: Evangelical Press). Both these volumes are highly recommended.

[2] Doubts have always been expressed about the authorship of 2 Peter and most modern scholars reject it as a composition of the apostle, in spite of its own claims. For a thorough defence of Petrine authorship, see Donald Guthrie, *New Testament Introduction*, 4th edition (Leicester: Apollos, 1990), pp. 805–42.

and try to learn more about how to communicate the message of salvation. Finally, we will sit at his feet, now an old man, in the opening verses of 1 Peter 5 and observe how to shepherd God's people. In each of these spheres—as disciple, preacher and pastor—he has a great deal to teach us and I hope that you will find his example as helpful as I have.

You may, of course, wonder why you should take time to read a book which deals largely with the duties of the ministry, whereas the relevance of a model of Christian discipleship is obvious to every believer. If you are not a preacher or a pastor, what value does Peter's contribution in these specialised areas have for you? Grateful as you may be for the leaders in your church, you feel no pressing need to learn more about what their work involves.

Such a reaction would be regrettable. For you do need to know the difference between good preaching and bad. You do need to be able to recognise competent pastoring when you find it. The church suffers when her members are unable to make these important distinctions. And one simple way of learning how to make them is to familiarise yourself with what God requires of men who hold these offices.

This is why God's instructions to preachers and pastors are given in the Bible, a book for all his people to read. God does not supply a secret manual intended only for professionals. The ministry has no 'trade secrets' to which the people in the pew are not admitted. Alexander Nisbet, a preacher in seventeenth-century Scotland, comments helpfully on the phrase 'The elders who are among you I exhort' (*1 Pet.* 5:1). He writes:

The duties of ministers and other office-bearers of the church ought to be pressed upon them in the hearing of the people, that so these officers may be the more engaged to their duty, and the people the more able to discern between those of them that are conscionable (conscientious) in the discharge of their duty and others that are not.[1]

You may be neither preacher nor pastor, but God wants you to understand something of what preaching should be like

[1] Alexander Nisbet, *An Exposition of 1 & 2 Peter* (Banner of Truth Trust, 1982), p. 189.

and what pastoring involves. In this way, you will know what to expect. You will be able to distinguish what is valuable from what is worthless, appreciating the one and avoiding the other. You will be able to pray more intelligently and sympathetically for the elders of the churches as they discharge their responsibilities. An informed people will always be an encouragement, not a threat, to true leaders. Their interest and understanding must surely produce a more devoted and enthusiastic ministry.

Peter will teach us about these matters. But we must begin where he did and where we all need to—as a disciple of the Lord Jesus Christ.

PETER THE DISCIPLE

2

A disciple like ourselves

Do you enjoy reading Christian biographies? I do, more often than not. There is something inspiring in accounts of lives committed to the Lord. As we read of surprising conversions, we are moved to pray more believingly for the salvation of those around us. Records of deep spiritual experience make us long for a similar transformation in our own hearts. Descriptions of high endeavour in the work of the kingdom broaden our vision and fill us with spiritual energy. Sufferings bravely borne for Jesus challenge us to carry our own crosses more cheerfully. To read the life of a George Whitefield or a Joni Eareckson is to be thrilled, rebuked, instructed and stimulated all at once. Biographies of God's people can be a delightful means of grace. Since we learn by imitation, living illustrations of what discipleship means are valuable in enabling us to follow Christ.

Yet not all biographies are so helpful. What can be more depressing, for example, than to read of the 'Christian superman'? He is someone who never fears, falters or fails. His life seems to be a catalogue of prayers answered and triumphs achieved. He is not in trouble as other men. No clouds darken his horizon and a tranquil smile never leaves his face. As we read of such a paragon, we feel more and more inadequate and discouraged. How could anyone hope to imitate such perfection? Or perhaps discouragement gives way to queasy irritation. The story is too sweet to swallow. He is simply too good to be true.

We do not, of course, want biographies which are destructive. The world is producing far too many of these already. The current fashion, dating from around the start of the twentieth century, is for what is called 'debunking'. This horrible term means that the task of the biographer is to expose all the hidden faults and shameful secrets of his subject. The underlying presumption is that there are no heroes. Every idol has feet of clay. Every cupboard must contain a skeleton. No-one has ever acted from disinterested motives, since honour is a sham and idealism no more than a cloak for self-advancement. The effect of this approach has been to imprison people in a bleak cynicism and to destroy hope and aspiration. When no-one is admirable, when all have been pulled down to the same low level, there is nothing left but self-disgust and mutual contempt. May we never descend to such a warped view of our fellow-Christians!

What we are looking for is a portrait of discipleship which will be at the same time inspiring and realistic. We need to read of those who have advanced beyond us in their experience of the Saviour and whom, therefore, we can safely follow. Yet they should not be so far beyond us that we cannot reach them. We must be able to identify with them, to feel that they are human beings like ourselves. Above all, we are looking for people who demonstrate in a striking way the character-changing grace of Christ.

We can do no better in this regard than consider the life of Peter. Here is an infallible, Spirit-inspired biography—truthful, balanced and helpful. The record of his relationship with Jesus provides us with a memorable illustration of what real discipleship involves.

The Gospels are full of Peter. No other disciple is mentioned so often, or has so much to say. No-one confesses Christ so boldly or argues with him so persistently. Peter is commended more highly than his companions and, apart from Judas, rebuked more stingingly. He is a jumble of contradictions—confused and clear-sighted, exasperating and lovable, boastful and humble, cowardly and courageous. Above all, he comes across as an intensely human figure. Of all the Twelve, his personality is most vividly drawn, so that he stands out from the others, a focus of our attention. We feel that we know Peter and can identify with him in both his strengths and his weaknesses.

This is precisely what God wants us to do. For Peter is not

portrayed in such detail simply because he was destined for future leadership. He is a living, breathing example of what it means to follow Christ. He is a prototype of discipleship. We can learn from his mistakes and try to imitate his virtues.

Although the story of his relationship with Jesus of Nazareth is complex and many-sided, three elements in Peter's experience stand out as especially relevant. He had a deep, personal commitment to the Saviour. Yet his discipleship was marked and damaged by persistent immaturity. Above all, he was someone who was chosen, shaped and protected by the Lord.

His story begins with the dawning of faith.

3

Becoming a disciple

What does the name 'Christian' mean? To whom does it refer? Some would answer that it applies to everyone who has been born in a 'Christian country'. When my wife and I lived in Athens many years ago, we discovered that our new friends all considered themselves Christians. It was an inescapable part of their national identity and they were surprised to be asked about their religion. 'Of course we are Christians!', they would say. 'What else could we be? Greeks are not Hindus or Buddhists!' Other people believe that they are Christians because they have been baptised, or confirmed, or are on a church membership roll. Still others think that being a Christian means going regularly to church or trying to do good to one's neighbour.

But these definitions are all inaccurate. Why? Because they miss the point of what being a Christian involves. They focus on nationality, ritual or human activity. But they say nothing about Jesus Christ. Yet he is at the centre of the faith to which he gave his name. Christianity apart from him is a meaningless '-ianity'. To be a Christian, or a disciple, to use the term found in the Gospels, is to be related to Christ in a most profound and personal way.

This truth was given classic expression in an answer given by Paul and Silas to a frightened man in a prison. Terrified by an earthquake, which had brought him close to ruin and suicide, he had asked them: 'Sirs, what must I do to be saved?' (*Acts* 16:30). Their reply was a simple one: 'Believe on the Lord Jesus Christ, and you will be saved, you and your household' (*Acts* 16:31). The Philippian jailer and his family did believe in Christ and, like millions ever since, they were saved. In other words, they became Christians.

'Believe on the Lord Jesus Christ'. Here is a perfect summary of what discipleship means. But to 'believe on' Christ involves more than accepting certain truths about him intellectually. That is included, of course, but saving faith is a commitment of our entire personality to the Saviour. We yield to him our minds, our hearts and our wills. Our lives depend on and revolve around the Lord Jesus. A disciple will trust, love and obey his or her Master. The relationship is, above all, intensely personal.

But it begins with faith and that is the means by which it is sustained. Peter was a disciple of Jesus because he was a believer in him.

Faith in Christ—'You are the Christ, the Son of the living God' (*Matt.* 16:16).

The circumstances of Peter's journey to faith are, inevitably, different from our own and we should not expect to find in his experience an exact pattern for conversion today. We have a completed gospel. At the time when he first met Jesus, Peter did not. The full message of the sinless life, atoning death and triumphant resurrection of Jesus of Nazareth can now be explained in its entirety to an unbeliever so that he or she, by God's mercy, may be brought to trust in the Saviour. They can hear the whole gospel at once. They do not need to wait for any further revelation. Whether their conversion happens quickly or over a more prolonged period, they have immediately available all the information they need in order to pass from death to life. To identify the moment of Peter's spiritual awakening is not so straightforward.

For he lived on the hinge between B.C. and A.D. His lifetime spanned Old Testament prophecy and New Testament fulfilment. There is every reason to think that he was a believing Israelite, trusting in the Lord's promises of salvation to his covenant people. In all probability he shared his brother's devotion to John the Baptist. Peter and Andrew, with their friends, would have been part of the godly remnant who were longing for the coming of the Messiah. This Messiah, when he arrived, revealed himself gradually and so Peter's faith developed in stages. He believed in Christ before Jesus had been crucified or raised from the dead. He believed before the outpouring of the Spirit on the day of Pentecost or the explanation of redemption in the New Testament epistles. His experience of Jesus was necessarily different from that of anyone today.

When was Peter converted? When were his sins forgiven? When did he pass from death to life? We simply do not know and this ignorance should make us wary of a simplistic approach which would treat his experience as a template for our own.

Yet we must not over-emphasise the differences. It would be a mistake to be misled by Peter's distinctive position in redemptive history into losing sight of the essential similarity between his faith and ours. For we are just like him in our sin and in our need. Enabled by the same Spirit, we exercise the same faith in the same Saviour. The Lord may have been revealed to us in a different way, but he is still 'Jesus Christ, the same yesterday, today and forever' (*Heb.* 13:8). In all that matters, Peter is an example of faith for every generation.

Before his public confession of Christ near Caesarea Philippi, his appreciation of the Lord had passed through several stages. He had been brought to Christ by his brother. John the Baptist had identified Jesus as the Lamb of God and Andrew, intrigued by this mysterious title, had spent time with the new teacher. His hours with Jesus had led him to a startling conviction which he was impelled to share, so 'He first found his own brother Simon, and said to him, "We have found the Messiah" (which is translated, the Christ). And he brought him to Jesus' (*John* 1:41,42).

'Found!' The verb speaks of a long search triumphantly ended. Archimedes, the Greek mathematician and scientist, is supposed to have made one of his greatest discoveries while sitting in his bath. Legend has it that he leapt from the water and ran into the street, shouting in wild excitement 'Eureka! I have found it!' But Andrew was telling his brother about a far more significant discovery. Here was the Lord's anointed, the hope of Israel, the deliverer for whose coming the people of God had been praying throughout so many centuries. These men could not yet have understood all that the title 'Messiah' would imply, but they knew at least that they had found the One for whom they had been waiting.

We see another dimension of Peter's faith in his reaction to a miraculous catch of fish on the Sea of Galilee. The Lord had commanded him to let down his nets in deep water. A lifetime's experience and an unproductive night's work suggested to the fisherman that this might be a pointless exercise, but he obeyed and was astounded at the result—so many fish caught as to fill two boats to sinking point. His response is significant. 'When Simon Peter saw it, he fell down at Jesus' knees, saying, "Depart from me, for I am a sinful man, O Lord!"' (*Luke* 5:8).

Here is a new level of awareness, more profound than the belief that the Messiah has appeared. For this incident convinced Peter of two important truths. He now saw in Jesus a majesty and power of which he had previously been unaware. There was something awesome about this person who could command the fish of the sea to do his bidding. He was more than a man; he was someone to be reverenced. In falling to his knees, Peter was acknowledging Christ's greatness and superiority. The 'Master' of verse 5 had become the 'Lord' of verse 8.

He also came to a new realisation about himself. 'Depart from me, for I am a sinful man, O Lord!' He did not really want Jesus to depart, of course. More than anything, he longed for his Master to stay. But he was now aware that he himself was unworthy of such a friendship. The sense of Christ's holiness was so overwhelming that Peter felt disqualified from remaining in his presence. 'I am a sinful man' was his despairing self-description. 'A sinful man'—not just partly, but pervasively sinful, guilty in his whole being.

Peter had seen Christ's holiness and his own sin. Without argument or excuse he confessed his unworthiness in an implicit plea for mercy. The Lord understood and responded in grace, as he will to every penitent: 'Do not be afraid' (5:10).

As the months passed, Peter's faith developed. The perfection of Jesus' sinless humanity must have made an unforgettable impact on his followers. Every additional miracle would re-emphasise his compassion and his power. His teaching, in public and private, would enrich their understanding and confirm to them that here was someone sent from God. But the full flowering of belief is first apparent in Peter's memorable declaration in the region of Caesarea Philippi.

The incident marks a watershed in the Lord's earthly life. His public ministry is drawing to a close. The shadow of Calvary is lengthening across his path. So he takes his disciples up into the high country, near the wooded slopes of Mount Hermon. It is a quiet place, ideal for teaching and reflection. He is planning to tell them about his approaching death and what it will mean for them. But he begins by asking them a question, the most important question which human beings can ever face or answer.

'Who do you say that I am?' (*Matt.* 16:15). Many opinions about Jesus are circulating in Galilee and Judaea. Some say that he is 'John the Baptist, some Elijah, and others Jeremiah or one of the prophets' (16:14). Others, bitter enemies, call him a glutton (*Matt.* 11:19) and a blasphemer (*Mark* 2:7). But what about the disciples? What is their view of Christ?

He has lived with these men and opened his heart to them. Will they stay loyal in the time of crisis? Only if they are persuaded about his identity. When he had walked on the water, they had cried: 'Truly You are the Son of God' (*Matt.* 14:33). When followers were deserting him in droves, Peter had said: 'You have the words of eternal life' (*John* 6:68). But were these firm convictions, for which they would live and die? Jesus is asking now for a definitive statement of what he means to them. Only such a commitment will carry them through the dark days to come. 'But who do you say that I am?'

Peter, impetuous and enthusiastic, answers for the group. His words fill his Master's heart with joy. His answer has echoed through history, repeated by countless believers. It is the only one which fits the facts. 'You are the Christ, the Son of the living God' (16:16).

'You are the Christ'. Andrew had been right. Peter is convinced that Jesus is the Messiah. He is the answer to Israel's prayers, the fulfiller of God's promises. He will be a prophet to teach them, a priest to pray for them and a king to rule them. More than that, he is the bringer of a new age. The Jews believed that when the Messiah came he would right all earthly wrongs and usher in the day of the Lord. The disciples see in Jesus this redeemer, expected over long centuries. He is the hope of the world.

[14]

But Peter has not finished. 'You are the Son of the living God'. On Jewish lips this is an astounding statement. If there was one truth above all others to which the Jews held most passionately, it was the oneness of the Lord God. Their daily confession of faith was: 'Hear, O Israel: The LORD our God, the LORD is one!' (*Deut.* 6:4). Several centuries earlier, thousands of their people had died under persecution rather than acknowledge any rival to Jehovah. To add another name to that of God was blasphemy and an abomination.

These words were, moreover, spoken in the area around Caesarea Philippi, a centre of pagan worship. In a cave nearby was the alleged birthplace of the Greek god Pan. Numerous temples had been built in that region to Baal, the Syrian deity. A white marble temple in the town was dedicated to the Roman emperor. Surrounded by such evidences of idolatry, any Jew would be filled with repugnance at the grossness of heathen images and with jealousy for the honour of 'the living God'. Here, if anywhere, his monotheism would blaze into a flame of holy intolerance.

Peter shares this faith of his fathers. But he and his friends have come to believe also that Jesus of Nazareth is related to the living God in a unique and intimate way. We cannot be sure how much he understood when he called Jesus 'the Son of God'. What did he know of the Trinity? Had he been taught about the eternal Son, creator of the universe? At any rate, he is acknowledging that their Master is different from all other men. He is more than the greatest of the prophets. He is God himself, God among men—Immanuel.

In his confession, Peter is pledging the disciples to serve this God and Saviour. They trust him with their whole beings. All their hope is in him, for time and for eternity. It is a statement of unreserved confidence, of saving faith. Here is the heart of Peter's discipleship—of all discipleship.

For, like him, we are surrounded by man's 'gods' and called to choose. The Lord Jesus confronts us, asking: 'But who do you say that I am?' What is our view of him? Is he the only hope of mankind? Is he the answer to our sin and lostness? Is he God and Saviour? If he is, then we must believe in him. We must place in him our entire confidence and depend upon him alone for all that we will ever need. Discipleship begins here. A Christian is anyone who has looked into the face of Jesus and said, 'You are the Christ, the Son of the living God'.

But, if faith is the essence of discipleship, it has two invariable companions. The first of these is the affection of the heart.

Love for Christ—'You know that I love You' (*John* 21:17)

Christ loved all his disciples, for 'having loved his own who were in the world, He loved them to the end' (*John* 13:1). But three were especially close to him—Peter, James and John. They alone accompanied him up the Mount of Transfiguration and into the Garden of Gethsemane. They were the inner circle, his dearest friends. Although John is honoured as 'the disciple whom Jesus loved' (*John* 21:20), Christ's love for Peter is also obvious throughout the Gospel narratives.

Peter, in turn, loved his Lord. We have seen that he reverenced and trusted him as God. But the majesty of Christ did not make him remote or unapproachable, for Peter's faith was warmed by human affection. He was drawn to Jesus. He cared for him, liked him, enjoyed his company.

But his love was not always wisely expressed. In fact, it was often misguided. He should not have contradicted Christ's prophecy of his death with the indignant 'Far be it from You, Lord; this shall not happen to You!' (*Matt.* 16:22). But he could not bear the thought of his Master suffering. When he protested, 'Lord, are You washing my feet?' (*John* 13:6), he was wrong. Yet he found it hard to watch Christ taking the place of a slave. Cutting off the ear of the high priest's servant (*John* 18:10) was a foolish action. But Peter wanted to protect Jesus from those who might harm him. Of course he was rebellious and rash. But these sins would never have been committed by a colder-hearted man. They are the flaws of an affection which may have been imperfect, but was nonetheless genuine.

For Peter, nothing was more important than being close to his beloved Master. 'Lord, to whom shall we go?' (*John* 6:68) was his response to the possibility of leaving Jesus, and we can hear the desolation in his voice at the very thought of going away. It is the echo of an older pledge of loyalty: 'Whom have I in heaven but You? And there is none upon earth that I desire besides You' (*Psa.* 73:25). We smile at his petulant question after Jesus had spoken of his going where Peter could not immediately follow: 'Lord, why can I not follow you now?' (*John* 13:37). He is like a child complaining at not being allowed to enjoy a privilege reserved for grown-ups. But it is love which his immaturity is expressing. There is an almost ridiculous extravagance in his reaction to John's quiet 'It is the Lord!' on the Sea of Galilee: 'Now when Simon Peter saw that it was the Lord, he plunged into the sea' (*John* 21:7). Absurd! Why get wet for the sake of a few minutes? Yet no one has truly loved who has never done, for love's sake, something silly and wonderful.

'Simon, son of John, do you love Me?' It was one question to which Peter, in spite of all his faults, could give an unhesitating answer: 'Lord, You know all things; You know that I love You' (*John* 21:17).

Yet, if love is not to degenerate into sentimentalism, it needs to be reinforced with the steel of action. Deeds, more than words, will prove its genuineness. 'If you love Me', said Jesus, 'keep my commandments' (*John* 14:15). So we find that Peter's faith was more than mental assent or emotional affection.

Obedience to Christ—'See, we have left all and followed You' (*Matt.* 19:27).

After an interval of two thousand years it is easy to forget how radical was the obedience which Jesus demanded from his first disciples. For we know what they did not—the end of the story. 'Come after Me, and I will make you become fishers of men' (*Mark* 1:17) was his summons. To us, these are the words of the Son of God, the One to whom all authority in heaven and on earth has been given. How could they do anything other than obey? He is calling them to a thrilling and privileged ministry. When the Lord himself commands, human beings are wise to yield.

Peter and Andrew, however, were listening to a village carpenter, turned unofficial religious teacher. Although convinced by this time that he was unique, they still knew comparatively little about Jesus and almost nothing about his future plans. Yet he was asking them to give up everything and follow him into the unknown. They were being called to abandon their home and livelihood, the security of the familiar, and to entrust themselves entirely to him. Here was a leap of faith indeed!

Amazingly, as it must have seemed to their contemporaries, they obeyed. Such was the impact of Christ's personality upon them that 'immediately they left their nets and followed Him' (*Mark* 1:18). This began a pattern of implicit obedience which Peter and his friends maintained to the end. From now on, Jesus was their Lord. They did what he told them, went where he sent them, accepted his instruction as their rule of life. At times they squabbled among themselves. They often misunderstood their Master and occasionally made foolish suggestions of their own. But Christ's authority over them was never questioned. In the final analysis, he was always in charge.

So when Peter reminded Jesus that 'we have left all and followed You' (*Matt.* 19:27), he was claiming no more than the truth. They had left all and followed Jesus. In the most practical way possible they recognised his lordship. It was an obedience which would continue until death.

For Peter, being a disciple meant devoting his whole being to Christ. Mind, heart, will—all were fully involved. He trusted, loved and obeyed his Master. His entire personality was surrendered to the Saviour.

Has the nature of discipleship changed since then? Surely not. Perhaps you are reading these pages as someone who is not yet a Christian. You may have wondered exactly what is involved in being a follower of Jesus. Peter has shown you. You need to believe in the Lord Jesus Christ, trusting in his perfect life and atoning death as the only basis for your acceptance with God. This faith will lead you into a life of obedience, where Christ's will is your law and pleasing him is your constant aim. Such obedience will be joyful, not a burden, because you will find yourself filled with an ever-increasing love for the Saviour who first loved you and gave himself for you.

To those who are Christians already, Peter's example is a reminder of the completeness of commitment which Christ requires. When our faith wavers, our love cools or we stumble in obedience, the life of this man, so far beyond us in his virtues yet so close beside us in his faults, calls us back to a wholehearted discipleship. Imperfect though our service will be, we need to show, as Peter did, that we have only one Master.

He illustrates also the glorious reality of friendship with Christ. For what jumps from the pages of the Gospels is the intensely personal nature of Peter's relationship with Jesus. We can lose this dimension so easily, without realising it. The church, religious activities, even the Bible can be misused to insulate us from the Saviour. We end up not really knowing him. We believe in him and obey him, yet he has become a stranger to us.

Yet Christianity is knowing Christ, not as a doctrine or an abstraction but as a real Person. Discipleship involves listening and talking to the Lord each day, keenly aware of the sound of his voice and of his ears open to our confidences and requests. We are to trust him, not as an insurance policy on which we may have to make a future claim but in the direct, immediate sense in which we depend on earthly loved ones. Obedience is meant to be far more personal than conformity to a code. It is doing something because this is what our beloved Master wants from us. To be a disciple means spending time in our Saviour's presence, not because we have to or because we want a favour but simply for the pleasure of his company.

One of the most striking characteristics of Christians of past generations was their intense delight in Jesus. C. H. Spurgeon is a notable example. In his autobiography he cannot keep from bursting again and again into heart-felt praise of his Saviour. Here is one example, chosen at random from among many:

I bear witness that never servant had such a Master as I have; never brother had such a Kinsman as He has been to me; never spouse had such a Husband as Christ has been to my soul; never sinner a better Saviour; never soldier a better Captain; never mourner a better Comforter than Christ hath been to my spirit. I want none beside Him. In life, He is my life; and in death, He shall be the death of death; in poverty, Christ is my riches; in sickness, He makes my bed; in darkness, He is my Star; and in brightness, He is my Sun. If there were no hereafter, I would still prefer to be a Christian, and the humblest Christian minister, to being a king or an emperor, for I am persuaded there are more delights in Christ, yea, more joy in one glimpse of His face than is to be found in all the praises of this harlot-world, and in all the delights which it can yield to us in its sunniest and brightest days.[1]

Has something gone missing in our modern Christian experience? Have we become too cerebral in our faith? Are we more respectable than devout? We have more tools available for Bible-study than ever before — Bible dictionaries, atlases and commentaries by the score. We can listen to taped sermons from almost any notable preacher in the world. Our everyday conduct may be above reproach, our Christian service diligent and conscientious. But where is our love for Jesus? Where is our passion for the Saviour? Do we speak and live as those who really know him? Or are our worship and witness being smothered under a blanket of impersonality?

Peter reminds us of the simplest of truths. A disciple is someone who knows and loves the Christ to whom he is committed. We cannot, as he did, accompany Jesus along the roads of Galilee. But we can know him just as intimately, as Peter himself confirms: 'Whom having not seen you love. Though now you do not see Him, yet believing, you rejoice with joy inexpressible and full of glory, receiving the end of your faith — the salvation of your souls' (*1 Pet.* 1:8,9).

Do you know a better definition of a Christian than that?

---

[1] C. H. Spurgeon, *The Early Years* (Banner of Truth Trust, 1967), pp. 95–6.

4

Continuing as a disciple

Receiving Christ in faith is not an ending but a beginning. For the word 'disciple' means 'learner'. It implies ignorance and a desire to be taught. Disciples of Jesus do not know everything. We have a great deal to learn and many changes to make. Our commitment may be sincere, but we are still immature and unstable and we will need the Master's help and guidance for the rest of our lives. This is the challenge of discipleship. It is the process by which a very imperfect person becomes more and more like his or her Lord. Discipleship holds in creative tension our natural weaknesses and our new identity, correcting the first and developing the second. In this respect, Peter is a particularly helpful example of what being a disciple means. His immaturities are on the surface and we can see clearly the process of change.

His first recorded words are typical of the man. Jesus has borrowed his boat as a floating pulpit and, after finishing preaching, has told him to move out into deep water and begin fishing. 'Master,' replies Peter, 'we have toiled all night and caught nothing; nevertheless at Your word I will let down the net' (*Luke* 5:5). Could there be a more perfect summary of his character? He obeys, but only after objecting. Christ's word prevails, but Peter is determined to have his say first. And this is merely the first of a series of incidents into which he will blunder, saying the wrong thing and showing in many different ways just how much he needs to learn.

He can be appallingly arrogant. After he had made his great confession that Jesus was the Messiah, the Son of the living God, 'from that time Jesus began to show to His disciples that he must go to Jerusalem, and suffer many things from the elders and chief priests and scribes, and be killed, and be raised again the third day' (*Matt.* 16:21). Here is a moment of high drama. The Lord is opening his heart to his followers, clarifying for the first time the essence of his mission. He has just explained to them his approaching rejection, death and resurrection. We might have expected them to respond with an awe-struck silence, at most a reverent question or two. Not Peter! 'Then Peter took Him aside and began to rebuke Him, saying, "Far be it from You, Lord; this shall not happen to You!" ' (*Matt.* 16:22).

Think of it! A sinner is rebuking the Saviour! A mortal man is presuming to take the Son of God to one side so that he can straighten out his thinking for him. It seems that Jesus is mistaken and that it is up to Peter to put him right, for he obviously believes that he knows better than his Lord. We are astonished at his impudence until we remember how often we have contradicted the Word of God with our own wishes. Is our sin so very different?

Shortly after this episode Peter displays his talent for compulsive talking. He, James and John are witnessing the miracle of the transfiguration. A heavenly glory is radiating from Jesus so that his face is shining like the sun and his clothes have become as white as the light. Moses and Elijah have appeared and are talking with him. Peter too has a contribution to make. 'Rabbi, it is good for us to be here; and let us make three tabernacles: one for You, one for Moses, and one for Elijah' (*Mark* 9:5). The proposal is crass enough in itself. But its foolishness is underlined by Mark's comment that he made this suggestion 'because he did not know what to say, for they were greatly afraid' (*Mark* 9:6). Peter, panic-stricken, spoke because he did not know what to say! It hardly inspires confidence in him as a future preacher.

On at least one occasion Peter shows more than a trace of self-centredness. The Lord has been explaining how hard it is for a rich man to enter the kingdom of heaven and Peter cannot resist drawing attention to the voluntary poverty of the disciples and what their sacrifice might deserve: 'See, we have left all and followed You. Therefore what shall we have?' (*Matt.* 19:27). When Christ begins to wash the disciples' feet, he is stubborn in his vehement protest: 'You shall never wash my feet!' (*John* 13:8). These are not attractive qualities.

Nor does anyone admire a boaster and Peter is boastful in his self-confident assertions of loyalty. He sees no need for Jesus' prayers that his faith will not fail under the assaults of Satan, for he says: 'I am ready to go with You, both to prison and to death' (*Luke* 22:33). Not even a specific warning that he is about to deny Christ that very night can shake his assurance: 'Even if I have to die with You, I will not deny You' (*Matt.* 26:35). Most poignant and terrible is his boast that 'I will lay down my life for Your sake' (*John* 13:37). What an irony! We can imagine a wistful smile on Christ's face as he takes up his disciple's words and fills them with a meaning Peter cannot begin to understand: 'Will you lay down your life for My sake?' (*John* 13:38). A life will indeed be laid down for others. But it will not be Peter's.

In the garden of Gethsemane we see the human weakness of the disciples. Jesus, entering his hours of agony, is distressed and sorrowful. He has brought with him Peter, James and John, shared with them something of his inner turmoil and asked them to 'Stay here and watch with me' (*Matt.* 26:38). He wants their support, yet even that is denied him, for 'He came and found them asleep, for their eyes were heavy' (*Matt.* 26:43). Yet shortly afterwards Peter is far too headstrong when he draws his sword and cuts off the right ear of the high priest's servant (*John* 18:10).

His lowest point is his cowardice in the courtyard of the high priest. Intimidated by servant-girls, he denies his Master three times with oaths and curses (*Matt.* 26:69–74). A few moments later he is weeping bitterly in the darkness, broken-hearted at the baseness of what he has done.

It was a chastening, life-changing experience. Yet not even this trauma was enough to purge Peter of his immaturity, for in the last chapter of the Fourth Gospel we see him driven by inquisitiveness. The risen Lord has been speaking about the future. He has prophesied that Peter will glorify God by a violent death. Yet Peter is not satisfied, but wants information about John's prospects as well: 'But, Lord, what about this man?' (*John* 21:21). Christ's response is a classic quashing of all such impudent curiosity: 'If I will that he remain till I come, what is that to you? You follow Me' (*John* 21:22).

Here then is a disciple who can be arrogant, talkative, self-centred, stubborn, boastful, weak, headstrong, cowardly and inquisitive. Not a pretty picture! It is an astonishing portrayal of one of Christ's closest friends. Why are these blunders included in Scripture? What is the purpose of a permanent public record of Peter's weaknesses? How can it be profitable for us to focus on the failings of a fellow-believer? Will this nurture the love which covers a multitude of sins? Are we meant to conclude that our shortcomings do not matter and that we can forget about any serious pursuit of holiness? Since even Peter was imperfect, can we lesser mortals settle back comfortably into a half-hearted obedience? By no means. His immaturity as a disciple is recorded for two immensely valuable pastoral reasons: to serve both as encouragement and as warning.

Encouragements from immaturity

The Gospel accounts of Peter's failures can encourage us in two ways.

Still a disciple: In the first place, they remind us that the presence of sin in our lives need not mean that we are not true followers of Christ. Peter is the acknowledged leader of the disciples. His imperfections are all too obvious. We might hesitate to welcome such a flawed personality as a prospective son-in-law. He would probably not be elected to office in our local church. Yet it is clear that he is genuinely committed to Christ and the Saviour, in turn, regards him with deep affection. Raw, foolish, exasperating—he is all of these and more. But he is a disciple, nonetheless. There are many like him.

We live, of course, at a time when popular Christianity is far too undemanding. Professing believers sit lightly to the requirements of God's law. Self-examination is criticised as morbid. Anyone who spent time in penitent heart-searching would be advised instead to visit a therapist and develop a healthier self-image. Grace seems cheap and a shallow assurance blinds many to their true spiritual need. So we do not want to encourage this superficiality by appearing to treat sin lightly. Yet it is possible, perhaps common in certain quarters, to go to the other extreme.

Some of God's people, often the most conscientious, are too hard on themselves. They find it difficult to believe that God has forgiven them for Jesus' sake. They may be intellectually aware that he loves and receives sinners in Christ, but they still have problems in coping with their own failures. They are not perfectionists, in theory at least. That is to say, they do not believe that it is possible for any fallen human being to live sinlessly on this earth. But they may be perfectionists in practice. They demand from themselves a standard which it is impossible to achieve and are mercilessly self-critical when they fail. In their anxiety to obey God, they unconsciously slide into legalistic religion, where salvation depends on performance.

In this atmosphere Christian joy is lost, replaced by a nagging sense of inadequacy. Haunting doubts arise. 'How can such a failure as I be a true Christian? If I am really born again, why do I give way to this particular temptation?' Peter brings us back to the cross. He is so obviously flawed as to remind us that we must be always and entirely dependent on the grace of God in Christ. He is so obviously genuine as to confirm that such grace is freely given. We will never be able to obey perfectly in this present life, never able to overcome all personal sin. But, as far as our standing with God is concerned, our failures do not matter! Jesus Christ has obeyed God on our behalf and has clothed us with his own righteousness. We can face without despair the evidences of our sinfulness, confident that we have a redeemer whose blood keeps on cleansing us.

As well as setting our hearts at rest, this awareness should make us more patient with our fellow-believers. It is easy to see the faults of other Christians and we are too often inclined to criticise or undervalue them. We may even doubt the reality of their faith. But if the Lord chose, honoured and used Peter, with all his faults, who are we to write off those who are strugglers like ourselves? A few years ago, there was a fashion among young Christians for wearing a badge with the letters BPWMPGIFWMY. The full message was: 'Be patient with me, please; God isn't finished with me yet'. We may not wear the badge, but we should never forget the plea. It is thoroughly biblical.

But growing: There is a second way in which we can be encouraged by the accounts of Peter's immaturity. The same Scriptures which record his failures tell also of his growth in grace. For the Peter whom we meet in the Book of Acts and in his Epistles is a changed man. He has developed, he has come of age as a Christian. Simon, the unsteady, has become Peter, the rock.

He still struggles, of course, and makes mistakes. We can hardly help laughing at his pompousness during the vision which came to him in Joppa. Hungry and ready for his midday meal, he sees an object like a sheet containing all kinds of animals, creeping things and birds. A voice from heaven tells him: 'Rise, Peter; kill and eat' (*Acts* 10:13). Peter is appalled! 'Not so, Lord! For I have never eaten anything common or unclean' (10:14). Here is the old Simon, arguing still, claiming that he is more religious than God. His principles, apparently, are too elevated to permit him to obey the voice of the Holy One!

More serious is his inconsistency at Antioch, where he is intimidated by a group of ultra-conservative Jewish Christians (*Gal.* 2:11–13ff). Before their arrival from Jerusalem he had happily eaten with Gentile believers in the new church, in disregard of ritual food laws. He now understood that, in Christ, such external regulations no longer served as barriers to fellowship. But he quickly abandons this Christian liberty under pressure from the narrow-minded. It is a serious betrayal of the gospel and, says Paul, 'I withstood him to his face, because he was to be blamed' (2:11). He may be one of the leaders of the church, but he is no more infallible than any other man, before or since.

Yet the overwhelming impression we obtain of the post-Pentecost Peter is of strength, wisdom, self-control. He is a powerful preacher (*Acts* 2:14–39), a humble servant (3:12), a courageous witness (4:19–20) and a joyful sufferer for Christ (5:40–42). His contribution to the Council of Jerusalem is weighty and persuasive (15:7–11,14). In his letters we see a tender, gracious pastor, ripe with the godliness of years, the light of heaven already shining from his face. The Holy Spirit has filled and transformed him. He is the same Peter still and yet how very different!

We too can expect to be changed, since God's 'divine power has given to us all things that pertain to life and godliness, through the knowledge of Him who called us by glory and virtue' (*2 Pet.* 1:3). We are not doomed to live with our immaturities for ever. The mighty Spirit is working within us, subduing our indwelling sin and making us more and more like the Saviour. We can expect to see in ourselves substantial and significant growth in grace. In this life, we will become more holy.

One of Satan's most powerful weapons is despair. He can so fill our minds with an awareness of our failings as to reduce us to hopelessness. Paralysed by a sense of inadequacy, we feel like giving up. We will never improve, we say, never overcome our besetting sins and innate weaknesses. 'But', says Peter, 'that is not true! Look at what I was—and then at what, by God's grace, I became. What Christ did in me he can do in you'.

What an encouragement! We need not make a peace-treaty with our sins or settle for second-best in our discipleship. God has given us his Spirit and provided us with the Bible, prayer, the sacraments, fellowship, suffering and other channels for his power. We must use these means of grace in the joyful expectation that, day by day, we will be changed from 'Simon' to 'Peter'.

Warnings against immaturity

We should not, however, let ourselves become too positive about Peter's immaturity as a disciple. Encouragements may be drawn from it, but sin is sin and always regrettable. Peter's failures were serious and damaging. He did not need to make these blunders and it would have been better for him if he had sought grace to avoid them. The record of his short-comings is a red warning light to all subsequent followers of Christ, signalling at least three dangers to which we may be subject.

We still sin: Peter reminds us that we do, and will, make mistakes. He was a committed follower of Jesus and yet he was frequently in the wrong. Even when well-meaning, and Peter almost invariably did mean well, he could act foolishly. Impelled by what he thought were the highest motives, he could be the mouth-piece of the devil. Sincerity is an inadequate protection against stupidity. To be a true disciple is no guarantee that we are always right. It is not enough to mean well or to be aiming in all honesty at what will glorify God. We are all so biased and liable to go astray.

It is easy to admit this in theory, as a doctrine of Scripture which we accept without hesitation. None of us would claim to have a monopoly of wisdom or to be always in the right. 'If we say that we have no sin, we deceive ourselves, and the truth is not in us' (*1 John* 1:8). We say 'Amen' to these familiar words and ask the Lord daily for forgiveness. But do we always live in the light of this truth which we profess to believe?

Christians are not noted for a readiness to admit that they have been wrong. We do not find it easy to ask brothers and sisters for forgiveness. We are not eager to receive loving correction. We tend to be touchy, stubborn and dogmatic. Our feelings are easily hurt and we then cherish a sense of injury, as if it were a precious jewel. The idea of an infallible pope is anathema to us, but we sometimes act as if we ourselves were above contradiction. We recognise, of course, that we are sinners, but woe betide the person who dares to identify one of our sins!

But true believers, acting for the best, can be seriously mistaken. We have seen that a high point of Peter's discipleship was when, near Caesarea Philippi, he confessed that Jesus was the Messiah (*Matt.* 16:16). The Lord pronounced him blessed and made him a glorious promise. Peter's heart was filled with love for his Master and a passionate longing to see him honoured. These noble emotions led him to reject with horror any idea that Christ would be killed. Never in his life had he a more lofty ideal; never did he speak more wicked words.

We know this because of the devastating response of Jesus: 'Get behind Me, Satan! You are an offence to Me, for you are not mindful of the things of God, but the things of men' (16:23). It is an electric, terrifying moment. Peter is told that he is being manipulated by the devil; he is doing Satan's work. Instead of a rock to build on, he is a stone to stumble over. If Jesus were to listen to Peter, his life's work would end in failure. Even though given in love, it is a searing rebuke. It lays all our self-confidence in the dust.

[28]

We should be more humble and less opinionated than we often are. We should be more tentative about our own ideas and readier to listen to others and to learn from them. In 1650, Oliver Cromwell was leading an English army in an unwanted war against the Presbyterians of Scotland. In most respects the two sides were very close, but certain issues had opened a chasm between them. On the third of August, Cromwell, in a famous plea to the ministers of the Kirk, asked them to think again: 'Is it therefore infallibly agreeable to the Word of God all that you say? I beseech you in the bowels of Christ think it possible that you may be mistaken'. Who was mistaken, Cromwell or the Covenanters? Opinions may differ, but no-one can doubt the general wisdom of the exhortation. Perhaps we should all practise saying, and meaning: 'This is what I think, but I could be wrong'. 'Yes,' comments Peter, 'you could; for I was, all too often'.

Our Achilles' heel: A second danger against which we need to be warned is the close connection which may exist between strength and weakness. We sometimes imagine that our vices are the polar opposite of our virtues. We can identify certain good qualities in our characters, strengths which we have reason to think we possess. There are also flaws of which we are painfully aware. It may seem to us that these are far removed from each other, with our personal pluses and minuses having nothing in common. But this may not be the case. Laughter and tears are apparent opposites, yet we can pass from one to the other in a moment. In the same way, our strengths and our weaknesses may be neighbours, not strangers.

A curious feature of the record of Peter's faults is that it sometimes brings a smile to our faces. His mistakes almost make him seem lovable. As we read of his blunders we feel a twinge of sympathy. Why is this so? Sin is not lovable. It is certainly nothing to smile at. Any child of God will find it repellent and ugly. Yet, even when Peter is wrong, appallingly wrong, we are not inclined to be hard on him. Judas disgusts us, but we cannot help liking Peter. Why? Is it moral blindness on our part? Have we a deficient understanding of the seriousness of sin? Perhaps, but another factor may be at work.

When Peter goes astray, his sin is not cruel or mean-spirited. He appears to be betrayed by his good qualities. Here is a natural leader, with an ardent temperament. He is a strong-minded man, passionate and enthusiastic. These are commendable characteristics. Yet the very same gifts could also make him impulsive and over-confident. His strengths became his weaknesses. His greatest personal assets often proved an Achilles' heel.

The incident of his walking on the water (*Matt.* 14:22–33) sums him up perfectly. In a sense, he looks ridiculous as he begins to sink beneath the waves of the Sea of Galilee. Why did he attempt something too hard for him? Why push himself forward into embarrassment and danger? Why not stay with the other disciples, where he was safe? Yet it was Peter's love for Jesus and confidence in his power that took him over the side of the boat. He ended up in trouble, but it was the trouble of a brave, affectionate man. We cannot be too critical of someone who fails because he attempts something beyond the vision of more timid and cautious disciples. He is always wading into water too deep for him, yet always turning back to his Master like a little child.

We are not excusing his sin. How much grief he caused his Lord! How much penitent agony he felt himself! How much harm he could have done as the mouthpiece of Satan! But his life seems to warn us that sin can be more subtle than we think. It is not always utterly vile. It can be more complex than such grossness as blatant disobedience or the indulging of unclean lusts. Sin is part of us, entwined in every aspect of our fallen humanity. It can fill our hearts with such deceitfulness that it spoils us at our best and enlists God's gifts in the service of evil. We need to be warned that Satan is devious enough to make use of not only our weaknesses but our strengths.

A man blessed with the ability to express himself fluently may be tempted to speak rashly. A woman's sympathy for those who are broken and hurting may make her too indulgent towards sin. Sensitivity may degenerate into self-pity; determination into stubbornness. The intelligent may misuse their minds to become arrogant or unbelieving instead of to love God. Warm-heartedness is a valuable quality, but not when it betrays us into temper tantrums.

We may covet the ability to remain calm under pressure, but such serenity sometimes freezes into callousness.

There is scarcely a gift which the devil cannot pervert. It is right that we should be loyal to all that is best in our Christian tradition. But when adherence to the old ways turns into blinkered conservatism, terrified of any change, it becomes a prison instead of a foundation. We are called to be intelligently aware of the world in which we live, like 'the children of Issachar who had understanding of the times, to know what Israel ought to do' (*1 Chron.* 12:32). Yet, studying the world too much can lead to conforming to it. Healthy commitment to the branch of the church to which we belong can turn into sectarianism. A love of seeing that all things are 'done decently and in order' (*1 Cor.* 14:20) can make us suspicious of genuine religious spontaneity and enthusiasm. The list of Satan's wiles is endless.

We should know our areas of weakness and pray for grace to overcome them. But Peter warns us also to guard against our strengths. An almost imperceptible lack of balance, a moment without the restraint of the Spirit, and we topple over into sin. At what area of competence might you be vulnerable? This brings us to the last and most solemn aspect of warning.

The weakness of our strength: We can fall most terribly at our strongest point. Peter's chief characteristic is his intense love for Jesus. His affection for his Master is his most winsome quality, patent throughout the Gospel narratives. If we had had to pick one disciple who would never deny the Lord, we would have looked to Peter. We can imagine him committing many sins, but never that of repudiating his Saviour.

Peter could not imagine it either. He was stricken by the warning of Jesus, doubly emphasised by the two opening phrases: 'Most assuredly, I say to you, the rooster shall not crow until you have denied me three times' (*John* 13:38). It is significant that, from this point on, he does not speak another word. Previously talkative, he is now silent. He sits in the upper room and goes out to the garden of Gethsemane as the acid of Jesus' words burns into his very soul. It etches inside him a determination that, no matter what happens, he will never deny his Lord. His feelings of loyalty build into a passion until, just before Christ's arrest, he has become a human time-bomb, primed to explode. When the soldiers move to seize Jesus, Peter's moment has come. Heart singing, he slashes with his sword, ready to kill and be killed. 'You were wrong, Lord!', he seems to be saying. 'Look at me now! I will lay down my life for your sake. Deny you? Never, never, never!'

Yet what do we find a short time later? 'The servant girl who kept the door said to Peter, "You are not also one of this Man's disciples, are you?" He said, "I am not"' (*John* 18:17). Then 'he began to curse and swear, "I do not know this Man of whom you speak"' (*Mark* 14:71). Oh, Peter! Mysterious. Awful. But so true to experience!

Each of us may be able to think of sins which we cannot imagine ourselves ever committing. God grant that we will not fall into them. We do not need to. But let us learn from Peter. Let us tremble and watch and pray. May the memory of our present confidence never come back to haunt us. 'Therefore let him who thinks he stands take heed lest he fall' (*1 Cor.* 10:12).

So far we have considered Peter's commitment to Christ and his continuing immaturity. But we have not yet touched on what is far and away the most important factor in the discipleship of Peter—or of anyone. It is that beside which everything else pales into comparative insignificance. Where is the Lord's place in all of this?

5

Chosen and kept as a disciple

There were many 'disciples' in first century Palestine. A disciple was the follower of any recognised leader, in philosophy, religion or politics. When a scholar, for example, began to gain a reputation for learning, he would attract a group of younger men who wanted to profit from his wisdom. The process was usually initiated by the student. He would select a teacher who particularly appealed to him or who lived nearby and ask if he could be accepted as a follower. The disciple chose his rabbi. But the relationship between the Lord Jesus and his disciples was different, as he makes clear in John 15:16: 'You did not choose Me, but I chose you and appointed you that you should go and bear fruit, and that your fruit should remain.' Here, Christ is in charge. He takes the first step. Instead of waiting for disciples to come to him, he selects and summons certain individuals for whom he has a definite destiny in mind.

In other words, discipleship begins with God, not man. To every believer he says: 'You did not choose Me, but I chose you'. We do not initiate the relationship. He does. The Lord's purpose for us is the foundation on which discipleship rests. This is a solid rock on which to build our own response of faith and obedience.

As we study Peter's experience, what impresses us most is something in which he plays no immediate part. We begin to see that he is a man caught up in a process far more wonderful than anything that he himself could have imagined. A mighty power is operating upon him, a power not constrained by anything which he may say or do. He is a man in God's hands. God has taken the initiative in dealing with him. From the beginning of his discipleship he is being guided by a sovereign will outside himself. Jesus Christ is shaping Peter, just as he shapes every one of his followers. We can identify seven ways in which he superintends Peter's discipleship, and ours.

i. Christ promises his disciple a new identity.

'Now when Jesus looked at him, he said, "You are Simon the son of John. You shall be called Cephas" (which is translated, A Stone)' (*John* 1:42). These are the Lord's opening words to Peter at their first meeting. It seems a strange beginning. Why does Jesus initiate the relationship with a prediction that his new disciple will have a name change from Simon to Cephas, the Aramaic equivalent of the Greek 'Petros'? Because, in those days, a change of name meant a change of nature. A person's name was more than an identifying sound or a group of letters. It was closely linked with his or her basic identity. This is true throughout Scripture. To 'call on the name of the Lord' (*Acts* 2:21) means to call on all that the Lord is in himself, not simply to utter his name in prayer. When, in the Old Testament, Abram became Abraham (*Gen.* 17:5–8) and Jacob, Israel (*Gen.* 32:28), these name changes signified a profound change in their characters. They had become different men.

Christ is telling this disciple that he too will be changed. He is now 'Simon'—rash, impulsive, unstable. But, as he follows Christ, he will become 'Peter', the stone—dependable and rock-like. This is not, moreover, simply a prediction. 'You shall be called Peter' refers not only to what Peter will become, but to what Christ has decided to do in and for him. It means: 'I know that you are Simon, but I will make you Peter'. It is a statement of the Lord's unalterable purpose for this man.

Jesus' message to every disciple is still the same, for, in this respect, Peter is no favoured exception. Christ observes us in all our present weakness and sin. Just as he 'looked at' Peter, and the verb refers to a deep, searching scrutiny, so he looks at us, discerning every facet of our beings. But what he sees does not disgust him or move him to despair. Rather, he speaks a gracious word of transformation, telling us who we shall become by his power. It is a thrilling and liberating promise. 'You will be called Peter'. He will make us into new people! This is his plan for us and he cannot fail to carry it out.

ii. Christ equips his disciple for service.

'Then Jesus said to them, "Come after Me, and I will make you become fishers of men" ' (*Mark* 1:17). Peter and Andrew are being called to the mighty work of catching human beings for Christ and pulling them to safety from the floods of judgment. It is an awesome task. How inadequate they must feel! How will they ever cope?

The answer is to be found in Jesus' precise division of responsibility. Their duty is to follow him—'Come after Me'. Let them concentrate on that. He promises in turn to equip and use them—'I will make you become fishers of men'. They do not have to make themselves into fishermen. They are not responsible for guaranteeing a catch. These are things which he has undertaken to do. If they follow Jesus, they can leave everything else in his hands. 'I will make you' is the ultimate and satisfying answer to all their inadequacies.

The church today is specialising in fishing techniques. Her focus of interest is in refining the details of evangelistic strategy and method. New rods and nets are promoted and various revolutionary types of bait are being developed for man-fishing. We are told that this is essential if we want a large catch. Yet, somehow, the new, improved nets are coming up as empty as the old.

The Lord points us in a different direction. 'You follow me', he says. 'Give yourselves to trusting me, obeying me, staying close to me, becoming more like me. Then you will find that I will equip and use you in ways beyond all your hope and imagining. Fulfil your own responsibility and let me take care of mine.'

We need to listen to our Master and to follow the priorities he sets for us. To so concentrate on what we are doing that we forget the Lord for whom we are supposed to be doing it, is a recipe for futility. Our ineffectiveness in evangelism is not primarily due to our lack of skill in fishing but to our lack of consistency in following. It has always been the case that the most Christ-like disciples have been the most useful.

[35]

iii. *Christ includes his disciple in his own ministry.*

'You are Peter, and on this rock I will build My church' (*Matt.* 16:18). Blood has been spilt over these words, church councils convened, countless books and pamphlets written. They are inscribed in gold letters on the vast dome of St Peter's in Rome and some ultra-Protestants seem to wish that the Lord had chosen another way in which to express himself! It is not our purpose here to enter the controversy.[1] The best way of approaching the passage is by trying to clear two thousand years of church history from our minds and asking ourselves what Jesus' words would have meant to those who first heard them.

It seems clear that he is speaking about Peter, who is the 'rock' referred to. It is equally obvious that he is not identifying him alone as the foundation of the church. As a matter of historical fact, Peter is the first of the Twelve to confess formally that Jesus is 'the Christ, the Son of the living God' (16:16). But he does so on behalf of his fellow disciples, not in splendid isolation. It is as their confessing representative that Jesus describes him as the rock on which the church will be built. Acts tells us that this is precisely what happened. The church of Christ was built on the testimony of the apostles, among whom Peter took a leading role. As he and his colleagues preached the gospel, they exercised the power of 'the keys of the kingdom of heaven' (v.19), opening the door of salvation to all who believed their message.

The point is that the Lord is here involving his followers in the work which he has come to earth to accomplish. 'I will build my church', he says. But he will not build it alone, by words of creative power. He will not convert sinners by direct revelation or angelic messengers. Instead, he will use people as his instruments. Peter, and all faithful disciples, will be part of what Christ is doing in the world. Our witness will be the construction material he will employ in building his church. We will have the satisfaction of knowing that our lives have a glorious purpose which stretches beyond time

---

[1] For a thorough modern treatment of the passage see D. A. Carson in *The Expositor's Bible*, vol. 8, F. E. Gaebelein, ed. (Grand Rapids: Zondervan, 1984), pp. 363–75.

into eternity. This is not our doing, but because of the graciousness of the Lord.

iv. Christ prays for his tempted disciple.
'Simon, Simon! Indeed, Satan has asked for you, that he may sift you as wheat. But I have prayed for you, that your faith should not fail; and when you have returned to Me, strengthen your brethren' (*Luke* 22:31,32). 'Satan has asked for you'. What a fearful prospect! The leader of the hosts of darkness has asked permission to place the disciples in his sieve to see if he can shake their faith out of them. They are going to be handed over for a time to the testing of the devil, that embodiment of cruelty and wickedness. One of his main targets will be Peter, the spokesman of the Twelve. Some dreadful experience will come upon him, searching him to the depths. How can he survive? To be 'asked for' by Satan would chill the courage and weaken the resolve of even the most steadfast.

Yet against this horror is set a mighty and glorious intercession: 'But I have prayed for you'. Blessed Lord Jesus! The Son of God has himself sought strength and mercy for his disciple. He has interposed his prayers between Peter and the malice of the enemy. Weak though he is, Peter is shielded by the supplications of Christ on his behalf.

That is why his faith will not fail. That is why Christ can speak with such assurance of Peter's future ministry 'when you have returned to Me'. Satan's testing will be overruled so that it results in good, not evil. The trial will not destroy Peter but strengthen him. The Lord will use the devil's sieve to serve a noble purpose. No disciple for whom the Saviour intercedes can fall to destruction.

He prays like this for every one of his followers. This means that, if we truly belong to Christ, none of Satan's attacks can finally overwhelm us. We may well tremble at the thought that we must 'wrestle against principalities and powers, against the rulers of the darkness of this age, against spiritual hosts of wickedness in the heavenly realms' (*Eph.* 6:12). But we need not fear, because Jesus is praying for us. His intercession is extremely specific. The word 'you' in 'I have prayed for you' is a second person singular: 'I have prayed for you as an individual. I have prayed for you by name'. Think of it! Even now your Saviour is praying for you personally, that you may be kept through temptation. 'Therefore He is also able to save to the uttermost those who come to God through Him, since He ever lives to make intercession for them' (*Heb.* 7:25).

v. Christ convicts his backsliding disciple of sin.

'And the Lord turned and looked at Peter' (*Luke* 22:61). We are now at the scene of Peter's denial. In verse 60 he is insistently denying any connection with Jesus. In verse 62 he is weeping bitterly in the darkness. What has made the difference? What has changed the cursing coward into the sobbing penitent? Something very simple, yet more profound than anything else on earth. 'The Lord turned and looked at Peter.'

What a look that must have been! More penetrating than a laser beam, more eloquent than ten thousand words. It was a rebuke, as the Lord looked beneath the bluster, reflecting in his eyes the awfulness of what Peter was doing. It was a reminder, for 'Peter remembered the word of the Lord, how He had said to him, "Before the rooster crows, you will deny Me three times"' (v. 61). He would remember also, perhaps, his fever-stricken mother-in-law, the miraculous catch of fish, the hand that had grasped him in the waves—all that had passed between him and the man whom he now claimed he had never known. Can we doubt that Christ's look was also a reassurance? In the crisis of his life, with Calvary coming near, he still had time to think about Peter. Was it the love shining unconquerably from those steady eyes that made the big fisherman cry like a baby?

The look of Christ brought Peter to himself. It broke his heart. It turned him from the far country to the painful, happy journey home.

Jesus still turns and looks at us in our backslidings. We do not deserve it. If he were to avert his face in holy loathing, we could have no complaint. But, again and again, when tempted or involved in sin, we feel his eyes upon us. Not literally, but when listening to a sermon or reading a verse of Scripture, in the face of a loved one, by a startling providence or simply the prompting of an awakened conscience. Somehow we become aware of Christ and are rebuked. We remember all that he has been to us and all that he has done for us. We are reassured that, unworthy though we are, he loves us to the end. His look melts our heart and brings us to repentance. Well may we pray:

> *Look upon me and be merciful to me,*
> *As Your custom is toward those who love Your name.*
> (*Psa.* 119:132,133)

vi. Christ reassures his fearful disciple.
'But go and tell His disciples—and Peter' (*Mark* 16:7). The days immediately following the crucifixion must have been among the darkest of Peter's life. His Master had died and been buried. On the night when Peter denied him they had exchanged a look, but had not spoken together. Peter had had no opportunity to tell Jesus how sorry he was or to ask for forgiveness. Now it was too late. He may have hoped that he had glimpsed mercy in the Lord's eyes, but he could not be sure. The memory of his sin filled him with guilt and haunting regret. Even the news of the resurrection, wonderful though it was, might not have been enough in itself to comfort him. Christ had risen, but would he want to have anything more to do with such a cowardly failure?

Knowing all this, the Lord sent to his fearful follower a special message of reassurance. The angel at the tomb on the first day of the week told the women to 'Go and tell His disciples that he is going before you into Galilee; there you will see Him, as He said to you' (*Mark* 16:7). But in that general promise were two specific words. They are found in no other Gospel. Only Mark, whose main source was Peter, records them. They are two words which Peter would never forget, inscribed on his memory in letters of gold: 'Go and tell his disciples—and Peter'. He alone is mentioned by name. Conspicuous in his sin, he is singled out for special reassurance. Jesus has not cast him off. Their relationship has not ended. He plans to meet his disciple again and summons him to the rendezvous.

In case this personal invitation might not suffice to overcome Peter's fears, he is granted a private meeting with the

Lord. What passed between them on that occasion we do not know. The other disciples told their friends that: 'The Lord is risen indeed, and has appeared to Simon!' (*Luke* 24:34). Paul simply states: 'He was seen by Cephas' (*1 Cor.* 15:5). But how amazing is Christ's grace! How intimate and tender his dealing with this bruised reed!

There are times when we too need personal reassurance, when our faith is too weak to grasp a general promise of help or mercy. So Jesus communicates with us individually. A verse of Scripture, perhaps read many times before, suddenly leaps from the page and grips us. We know that the Lord is speaking directly to us. That verse is meant for us, as surely as if our name were spelt out in it. It may be a promise of forgiveness, strength or guidance. It may be a confirmation of Christ's love. But it is the message we need and, at that moment, for us alone. 'Go and tell His disciples—and Peter'. How often God has included our names in his Word!

vii. Christ restores his disciple to fellowship and usefulness.
'Simon, son of Jonah, do you love me more than these? Feed My lambs' (*John* 21:15). The last major episode in this stage of Peter's discipleship is described in the final chapter of the Gospel according to John. Soon the Lord will initiate the teaching process (*Acts* 1:3) which will prepare his followers for the coming of the Spirit and a new era in their ministry. First, however, he must restore Peter. The incident of his denial has not yet been dealt with. There is unfinished business to be settled between Christ and his damaged disciple. Fittingly, the fisherman is re-commissioned at the sea-shore, where he first heard the call to service.

Once again, it is clear that the initiative rests entirely with Jesus. The disciples seem directionless. As commanded, they have travelled to Galilee. But they are at a loss as to what they should do next, so Peter takes the lead in opting for the comfortably familiar: 'Simon Peter said to them, "I am going fishing". They said to him. "We are going with you also"' (*John* 21:3). Their fishing, however, is unproductive, leaving them bewildered and discouraged.

Suddenly, Jesus appears and all is changed. In a reprise of an earlier miracle, he fills their net to bursting. A charcoal fire has been lit for warmth and cooking. As he had once served them by washing their feet, so he now prepares an early breakfast of fish and bread. Filled with awe, they eat in silence. No-one dares to address the Master, now clothed with new mystery. When the meal has ended, he speaks to Peter, the focus of his immediate concern.

Jesus' questioning is gentle but relentless. Three times, by the fire in the courtyard of the high priest, Peter had denied his Lord. Now, beside another fire, he is again asked three times about his relationship with Christ. Each question makes him relive the bitterness of his betrayal. Yet each trembling profession of love wipes out, as it were, one of the stains of cowardice.

He is humbler than he once was. His love for Jesus is no greater than that of the other disciples. He does not love as purely or unselfishly as he should. But he does love his Lord and, when driven almost to desperation by the insistence of the interrogation, he can do nothing but cast himself upon Christ's perfect knowledge of his heart: 'Lord, You know all things; You know that I love You' (21:17). It is enough. Repentant and restored, he is appointed again to service— the care of Christ's sheep.

We shall see in later chapters how Peter fulfilled his pastoral responsibilities. But the point to notice here is that his restoration to usefulness is entirely the Lord's doing. It is Jesus who meets him, examines him and enables him to make a fresh start. Peter himself may have despaired of ever again being allowed to serve his Master. But what matters is that the Lord had plans for Peter and these he implemented in his own time and way. When we fall into sin, as we do, we cannot restore ourselves to God's favour or presume to reclaim a place among his servants. For this we are entirely dependent upon the gracious initiative of Christ.

We should have obtained by now a clear impression of Christ's role in Peter's discipleship. Quite simply, it is all-important. Whatever word we choose to express the overwhelming nature of the Lord's influence—basic, fundamental, determinative—it is plain that Peter is a man in the hands of God. He is a piece of clay, being shaped into a vessel designed for an honourable destiny. Every detail of his life has been foreordained. Even the moment and manner of his death are fixed in the divine programme (*John* 21:18,19). He is and will be what Christ has planned. His own actions are significant, of course. But what ultimately matters is the Lord's purpose for him.

There is nothing more vital to understand than this about our own discipleship. We are not in any way to minimise personal responsibility. Our duties are many. We are called to believe, pray, study, obey, work, wait and suffer—all of these, and more. We will be rewarded for our faithfulness and disciplined for disobedience. Every word we speak has an eternal impact, every action is pregnant with more significance than we can grasp.

But what is the determining factor in our discipleship? Not our faith or devotion, but the fact that God has chosen us to be his. Before the universe was made he set his love upon us. In unfathomable grace, the triune God has decreed to save us, make us perfect, bring us to glory. The Father gave us to the Son, who has enlisted us in his service for ends and reasons of his own, of which we are only dimly and partially aware. The course of our lives has been planned in advance. Everything we do and experience is part of a vast tapestry which he is weaving. We are caught up in something far bigger than we can understand. God has decided to make us like his beloved Son and the irresistible power of the Holy Spirit is now at work within us with that goal in view. The only reason we will persevere in faith, and we will if we have been born again, is because God will persevere with us.

This awareness should grip and master us. 'If God is for us'—and he is—'who can be against us?' (*Rom.* 8:31). Since he has decreed glory for his disciples, nothing else matters. We are weak in ourselves. Strong powers are arrayed against us. We may be feeling dispirited and downcast. But none of this matters! What matters is that Christ has taken every disciple to his heart and written 'Mine' upon us. 'You did not choose me, but I chose you and appointed you that you should go and bear fruit, and that your fruit should remain' (*John* 15:16).

The biblical doctrine of election can be made to appear cold and abstract, remote from everyday living. But it is nothing of the sort. As we think of our discipleship, it fills us with an abiding peace. For it reminds us that our commitment to Christ was God's idea long before it was ours. What he has decreed, he is responsible for carrying out.

What a joyful truth! We can relax and rejoice in the Lord's sovereign purpose. We can go forward into the Christian life with unhesitating confidence in our God. We do not need to be afraid. There is no-one who can pluck us from the Father's hand. Peter, above and beyond everything else, was a man who was chosen, mastered, shaped and used by Christ. So are we. For that is what a disciple really is.

'The Lord will perfect that which concerns me; Your mercy, O Lord, endures forever; Do not forsake the works of Your hands ... For we are His workmanship, created in Christ Jesus for good works, which God prepared beforehand that we should walk in them' (*Psa.* 138:8; *Eph.* 2:10).

PETER THE PREACHER

6

A master-preacher

There is no greater need today than for powerful preachers of the gospel. Unless men and women call on Jesus Christ for salvation, they will be condemned to hell. But 'how shall they call on Him in whom they have not believed? And how shall they believe in Him of whom they have not heard? And how shall they hear without a preacher?' (*Rom.* 10:14). Able preachers are pitifully few. In cities of millions there may be no more than one or two such men. Whole regions have no opportunity to hear the message of salvation. We are experiencing a fulfilment of the Old Testament warning: 'Behold, the days are coming, says the Lord, That I will send a famine on the land, Not a famine of bread, Nor a thirst for water, But of hearing the words of the Lord' (*Amos* 8:11).

Many speak from pulpits—but they do not preach the gospel. They suggest that their hearers try to be good. They recommend self-fulfilment and getting rid of inhibitions. They may offer whimsical comments on current events or new-age spirituality with a Christian veneer. Some choose to ridicule the supernatural or attack the absolutes of God's law. But there is no declaration of what God has done in Christ for the salvation of the lost. There is not a word of grace or of real hope. Their poor people listen in ignorance and die in their sins.

Some do preach the gospel—but not powerfully. These are good men, eager to be faithful. They have trusted Christ for themselves and know that they are commissioned to proclaim him as Saviour to others. But most of their regular listeners are professing Christians and there seems little point in telling them again what they already know. So the gospel

[47]

tends to be tacked on to sermons which are designed primarily for believers. It becomes the predictable formula with which every message closes. The idea is that, if a casual visitor attends the service, enough information will be provided about salvation to enable him or her to come to faith. But no-one really expects this to happen. Many ministers will admit that they feel more comfortable in teaching Christians than when they are preaching evangelistically. This awkwardness is reflected in their sermons and they communicate the gospel in a hesitant and ineffective way.

Few of us, indeed, are skilled at evangelistic preaching. But instead of lamenting our weakness we should set about correcting it. Nothing is more helpful in this regard than the bracing influence of a good example and no better model can be found than Peter, the preacher.

Seven of his public addresses are recorded for us in Acts, as well as the brief address given by 'Peter and the other apostles' on their second appearance before the Sanhedrin (5:29–32). This is a considerable amount of material—and it is infallibly recorded. The apostle has not been misunderstood or misquoted. No careless reporting has distorted his message. Instead, the Holy Spirit has inspired Luke to present us with the very words—and the most crucial of these— which came from Peter's lips as he preached in Jerusalem and Caesarea.[1]

Some great preachers have left little permanent record of their work. We can read of the notable effects of their ministries and of the high esteem in which they were held by their contemporaries. But we can make no assessment for ourselves, for their sermons were not written down and so died with them. In Peter's case, however, a substantial transcript has survived and we know exactly how he preached the gospel.

His is the earliest—and thus definitive—preaching. The risen Christ has just told Peter and the others that 'you shall receive power when the Holy Spirit has come upon you; and you shall be witnesses to Me' (1:8). It is under the

---

[1] For a defence of the conviction that 'Peter . . . said to them' (2:14) means precisely what it says, see the Appendix.

control and in the energy of this divine Spirit that Peter preaches. The realities he speaks about are freshly impressed on his consciousness. He is not delivering a message which philosophers have adulterated or heretics have distorted. His preaching is not stale, an attempt to rekindle the embers of an enthusiasm which long years have all but extinguished. This is new-minted and white-hot gospel preaching; preaching as it is meant to be. This is the prototype, the real thing.

What is more, it was astoundingly effective. After Peter's sermon on the day of Pentecost, 'those who gladly received his word were baptized; and that day about three thousand souls were added to them' (2:41). His preaching in Solomon's porch made such an impact that 'many of those who heard the word believed; and the number of the men came to be about five thousand' (4:4). The Jewish religious leaders, arrogant and hostile though they were, 'marvelled' at his forcefulness (4:13). As he brought to a conclusion his message in the house of Cornelius, 'the Holy Spirit fell upon all those who heard the word' (10:44).

Such responses are phenomenal. A man stands up and speaks and hearts are broken, lives changed and repenting sinners flood into the kingdom of heaven. Words from his mouth are the instrument by which thousands are delivered from death to everlasting life. As the Spirit's spokesman, Peter achieved more in an hour than most of us will accomplish in a lifetime. Here is gospel ministry in all its majesty and power. How many of us have experienced anything like it? If only we could learn from him, catch some sparks of the fire with which he preached! We cannot afford to neglect such an example.

He does not, of course, provide us with a complete blueprint for evangelistic ministry. He was speaking to Jews and God-fearers after all, audiences familiar with the Old Testament Scriptures. If we wished to make a comprehensive assessment of apostolic evangelism, we would have to include Paul's ministry to pagans in such places as Lystra and Athens (14:15–17; 17:22–31). We would also need to cover other aspects of Peter's preaching. Was there, for example, a basic framework around which every message was constructed? If

[49]

so, what was it? That is a complex issue which would take us far beyond the scope of this book.

But, focusing upon his four main evangelistic sermons—at Pentecost (2:14–39); in Solomon's porch (3:12–26); before the Sanhedrin (4:8–12); and in the house of Cornelius (10:34–43)—we can identify five characteristics of Peter's preaching which are often lacking today. They are: relevance, Christ-centredness, boldness, a readiness to preach the demands of grace and a dependence upon the power of the Holy Spirit. If we want to improve as gospel preachers, we need to take lessons from this master-craftsman.

1. Relevance
2. Christ centredness
3. Boldness
4. Preach demands of Grace.
5. Dependance on Holy Sp.

7

Relevant preaching

Relevant. What an intimidating word! It is the non-negotiable demand of our impatient age. 'What is the point? What has this to do with me?' These are the questions asked by a society in a hurry. Bombarded by information on every side, the average attention span can be measured in seconds. Communicators in politics, commerce and culture know that they must tap instantly into the concerns of their audience. If not, they will be ignored. People are interested only in what they perceive to be of immediate practical benefit. They have no time for abstractions or theorising. To appear irrelevant is the kiss of death.

The church, considered antiquated to begin with, faces this pressure in an intensified form. It is dismissed as hopelessly remote from real life, with the quaint ordinance of preaching especially redundant. A preacher, therefore, feels that, if he is to be heard at all, he must be seen to be incisively up to date. His sermons should be at the cutting edge of culture, reflecting issues as current as those in the morning's newscast. If Christians want the privilege of the world's attention, we are told, our preaching must deal with the issues of today. If we do not speak to the interests of the man in the street, we will neither receive or deserve a hearing, because we have nothing relevant to say.

Some evangelicals have capitulated to this demand and become obsessed with relevance. They do not abandon the gospel. Indeed, they often show commendable enthusiasm for reaching the lost with the message of salvation. But they have been influenced by the ethics of consumerism, where the customer is always right. They describe themselves, with some satisfaction, as 'seeker-centred'. In other words, their ministry is shaped by the felt needs and interests of the audience. The pew is allowed to dictate what message comes from the pulpit. They are saying, in effect, to unconverted people: 'Tell us where you hurt or what you hope for and we will show how Christ can satisfy your needs'. In this way, they believe, the gospel will be seen to be relevant and will attract an ever-wider hearing. There is more than a grain of truth in this, but the price of such accommodation to market forces is appallingly high.

Other Christians are disgusted by this because they see it as a pandering to the wishes of the world. Unbelievers are dead in sin and can neither understand nor take an interest in the gospel. Until they are given new life by the Holy Spirit nothing from the Bible will make sense to them. When the Spirit does work, they will inevitably repent and believe. What point, then, is there in bending over backwards to win a hearing? Why should we take trouble to speak in a contemporary idiom to those outside? All that is necessary for the salvation of the elect is that we proclaim the truth and rely upon the power of God.

This approach is based on some elements of a sound theology. But it is also an overreaction. There is no merit in deliberate obscurity. Pride in being incomprehensible is almost as bad as an addiction to modernity. When remoteness from everyday concerns becomes a badge of faithfulness, something is far wrong. A preacher who begins his sermon with the words, 'Today we continue our study of the doctrine of the atonement' still has a lot to learn about communicating.

Where can we find a scriptural balance between trendy, shallow preaching and preaching which is out of touch with the interests of ordinary people? Peter provides a perfect example. His ministry is as relevant as it is faithful, and vice versa.

What strikes us at once in his four evangelistic sermons is that, in every case, he begins with what is of immediate interest to his hearers. The Pentecost crowd in Jerusalem is fascinated and perplexed by the spectacle of Palestinian Jews speaking in foreign languages. 'Whatever could this mean?' they ask (2:12). Some sarcastically suggest that the speakers are full of new wine (2:13). Here is the point of contact upon which Peter seizes with unerring timing and a possible touch of humour: 'These are not drunk, as you suppose, since it is only the third hour of the day' (2:15).

A beggar, lame from birth, has been a regular fixture at one of the temple gates. His miraculous healing causes a sensation and provides an opportunity for evangelism. How does Peter begin? 'Men of Israel, why do you marvel at this, as though by our own power or godliness we had made this man walk?' (3:12). When brought before the Sanhedrin, his starting-point is identical: 'If we this day are judged for a good deed done to the helpless man, by what means he has been made well . . .' (4:9).

Peter's acceptance of an invitation to the home of the Roman Cornelius is an epoch-making event. Centuries of racial separation are being swept away. Both Jews and Gentiles in that house must have been conscious of the novelty of their meeting together. How is it possible for the chosen people to associate so closely with 'dogs' from the nations? So the apostle, when invited to speak, does not begin with sin or guilt, grace or salvation. 'Then Peter opened his mouth and said: In truth I perceive that God shows no partiality' (10:34).

There can be no doubt that, in every instance, Peter has captured the attention of his audience. He is speaking about the very topics in which they are currently interested. They do not have to make an effort to tune in to the preacher's wavelength. His words are in immediate accord with what they have been thinking about. 'Here is a really relevant speaker', they would have said to themselves. 'He is going to tell us exactly what we want to know'. They are gripped, compelled to listen. A good beginning for any preacher! But what is far more significant is what Peter does next.

He moves quickly in every sermon from what interests them to what interests him—and that is the Lord Jesus Christ. Note how directly and speedily he introduces the Saviour: 'Men of Israel, hear these words: Jesus of Nazareth . . .' (2:22); 'The God of Abraham, Isaac and Jacob, the God of our fathers, glorified his Servant Jesus . . .' (3:13); 'Let it be known to you all, and to all the people of Israel, that by the name of Jesus

Christ of Nazareth . . ' (4:10); 'The word which God sent to the children of Israel, preaching peace through Jesus Christ—he is Lord of all . . .' (10:36). After the attention-grabbing introduction, he at once begins to proclaim Christ. But we need to think carefully about how these two elements of his sermons are related.

His opening statements are not gimmicks. This is not the verbal trickery of the salesman who pretends to share our interests only in order to manipulate us in the direction which suits him. The cultist who has knocked on our front door may begin by commenting on our delightful children, manicured lawn or the unseasonably fine weather. What could be more timely? But he is interested in none of these things. They are merely conversational hooks, designed to pull us into a dialogue which he will use to bring us to his real agenda. In other words, there is no significant connection between the cute introduction and the content of what he intends to say.

Preachers, without realising what they are doing, sometimes resort to such confidence tricks. A middle-aged man addressing a group of young people begins by referring to a current pop star about whom he obviously knows nothing. Or perhaps he tries to spice up his language with a piece of teenage slang. Eager to establish credibility, he has merely made himself seem foolish. A message starts with glittering promises of immediate benefits. But the promises are never developed and those initially attracted are left feeling cheated. A catchy reference to some current event is so obviously unrelated to what follows that discerning hearers feel contempt for the stratagem designed to catch their attention. This is not relevant preaching. Such devices are, rather, the trinkets offered by those 'peddling the word of God' (2 Cor. 2:17).

Peter, however, is genuinely interested in the topics with which he begins. He is not simply using them as clever bids for attention. He takes them seriously and intends to explain them. But his main commitment is to proclaiming Jesus Christ as the only answer to all the needs of his hearers. How then does he link introduction and message? It is by showing the connection between their interest and his. He makes plain that what they are thinking about is a pointer to the great, vital issue which they need to consider and about which he is speaking.

The people on the day of Pentecost are fascinated by the phenomenon of speaking in tongues. Peter shows that this has been caused by the long-promised outpouring of the Spirit, who in turn is the gift of the exalted Jesus (2:16–22). Their interest in tongue-speaking, although they did not know it, is in fact an interest in something very closely connected with Jesus Christ.

Both the crowd and the religious leaders are astounded by the healing of the lame man. But Peter points out that this miracle is due to the activity of the Saviour, crucified and risen, and that 'His name, through faith in His name, has made this man strong, whom you see and know' (3:16); 'by Him this man stands here before you whole' (4:10). Without realising it, they are enthralled by the mighty work of Jesus.

Cornelius and his fellow-Gentiles are puzzling over Peter's willingness to come among them and his surprising statement that 'God has shown me that I should not call any man common or unclean' (10:28). What can he mean? The answer to their dilemma is to be found in Jesus and in the fulfilment of the prophetic witness that 'whoever believes in Him', whether Jew or Gentile, 'will receive remission of sins' (10:43). He is the One through whom it is now plain that 'God shows no partiality' (10:34).

The pattern therefore is always the same. Peter relates his preaching to his hearers on two levels. It is obviously and instantly relevant in that he begins with whatever issue is concerning them. But, more importantly, it is truly and eternally relevant in that he uses this focus of interest to lead them directly to Christ. They may not initially be interested in the Son of God. But he is the One towards whom Peter invariably and exclusively directs their attention. Speaking to different people and in varying situations he always begins at the place where he finds his audience, then traces from there a direct road to Jesus.

What is he teaching us?

He is reminding us that there is nothing wrong with taking as our starting-point in preaching the felt needs and pressing concerns of our hearers. Indeed, this is a wise procedure. When speaking to believers we may be able to dispense with a striking introduction and plunge straight into an exposition of our subject. Our hearers, we may hope, are interested before we begin. We should not need to capture their attention, because they are already eager to understand the Scriptures. Ravenous for that Word which is the food of their souls, they have no need of an appetising hors d'oeuvre to whet their appetite. (Oh, if only! groans the discouraged pastor!)

When preaching the gospel, however, we are consciously addressing those who have little interest in the message of salvation. So we have to win their attention, persuade them that what we have to say is of the utmost relevance to their lives and destinies. We must take pains to begin where they are. The Spirit, who alone brings men and women to repentance and faith, has chosen to use means and one of the most fruitful of these is the skill of the speaker in capturing the interest of his listeners.

C. H. Spurgeon, a giant among preachers of the gospel, understood well the importance of this initial point of contact:

Their attention must be gained, or nothing can be done with them . . . We must make the people feel that they have an interest in what we are saying to them . . . I never did hear of a person going to sleep while a will was being read in which he expected a legacy, neither have I heard of a prisoner going to sleep while the judge was summing up . . . Self-interest quickens attention.[1]

In the twentieth century, D. Martyn Lloyd-Jones, renowned for thorough, detailed biblical exposition and for his distaste for gimmicks of any kind, makes the same point, not just in the context of evangelism but about preaching in general:

This question of relevance must never be forgotten . . . The preacher is a man who is speaking to people who are alive today and confronted by the problems of life; and therefore you have to

[1] C. H. Spurgeon, *Lectures to My Students* (London: Marshall, Morgan & Scott, 1976) pp. 127, 138–9.

show that this is not some academic or theoretical matter which may be of interest to people who take up that particular hobby, as others take up crossword puzzles or something of that type. You are to show that this message is vitally important for them, and that they must listen with the whole of their being, because this really is going to help them to live.[1]

So much gospel preaching today is predictable and unimaginative. It begins in a theoretical, abstract manner to which ordinary, unchurched people simply cannot relate. They do not see the relevance of what is being said. They are not made to see it. It does not appear to touch their lives in any meaningful way. Mild interest soon gives way to bewilderment and boredom. They are turning away from the gospel, we say. Perhaps, but it may be that what they are rejecting is a dry, tedious presentation of the most thrilling message in the world.

We cannot help people who are not listening to us. So we must do everything we can to compel them to listen. We must make it our goal to command their attention. This will mean entering their thought world and trying to imagine what would interest us if we were in their place. The true preacher is filled with a passionate determination: 'I will be heard. I will make you understand why the gospel is important for you. You may reject the message I bring, but you will never be able to say that it was irrelevant'. This is why Peter began his sermons as he did and why we should follow his example.

But, having done that, we must at once bring the people to Christ. Our starting-point has been what interests them. But we dare not pause there. We must, at all costs, avoid giving the impression that our preaching is governed by their demands and felt needs. They are not in charge of the process. They are not in a position to dictate the agenda and can never be allowed to do so. Otherwise, they will be in completely the wrong frame of mind for hearing the gospel.

Any preacher worthy of the name longs to preach relevantly, to bring messages which meet the needs of his hearers. If not, what is the point of preaching at all? But, come to think of it, why are we preaching? Why is it necessary to convey

---

[1] D. Martyn Lloyd-Jones, *Preaching and Preachers* (London: Hodder & Stoughton, 1971), p. 76.

gospel information to those who are not believers? Surely it is because they are not aware of their real needs. They are ignorant of those very truths which are most relevant for them. This is part of what being 'lost' means. The lost do not know where they are, or where to turn. Their sense of direction is distorted. They are confused, helpless, frittering away their years on trivialities. In the light of sin and judgment, heaven and hell, their whole course of life is a tragic irrelevancy.

This means that, if we allow the unconverted to tell us what they need, we are by that very action rendering ourselves unable to help them. It would be a case of inviting the blind to lead those who can see. For they do not know what they need. They may think that they know. They may be very dogmatic and assured about what their needs and problems are. But they are invariably mistaken.

Here is the fatal weakness of the 'seeker-centred' approach. 'Tell us what you want,' such churches say to enquirers, 'and we will show you how Christ can provide it'. But what people want is rarely what they should want, and to allow the sick to prescribe their own medicine is not relevant but cruel. A physician would be incompetent indeed who permitted patients not only to describe their symptoms but to suggest a diagnosis and outline the treatment required. It would be a betrayal of professional responsibility. Doctors exist because people do not know what is wrong with them or how they may be cured. Gospel preachers exist for the same reason.

We should not be intimidated by the modern clamour for relevant preaching. The fact is that it is only the message of salvation that is relevant. We stand up and look at all the different individuals who form the congregation we are about to address. Many of them may be strangers to us. We do not know their names, their backgrounds, their personalities, their circumstances, their present problems or their conscious expectations. How then can we preach relevantly? Because we do know what they need. We are far more aware than they are of what is relevant to them and it is our task to provide it. 'Find the hurt and heal it,' advise the experts in sociological analysis. But we already know what the hurt is— the mortal wound of sin.

The urgent need of every one of our unconverted hearers is salvation. They need to have their sins forgiven. They need to be reconciled with God. They need to turn in sorrow from their godlessness and to call on the Lord Jesus for mercy. They need Christ. It does not matter whether they are old or young, rich or poor, educated or uneducated, black or white, outwardly moral or in the gutter. 'There is no difference; for all have sinned and fall short of the glory of God' (*Rom.* 3:22,23). There is only One who can help them and we have come to proclaim the astoundingly good news that he offers himself now as their Saviour. This is the message of the gospel—universally, currently, eternally relevant—which is entrusted to us.

Let this persuasion master us. In the gospel we have what people need more than anything else in the universe. Nothing matters more to our hearers than that they should understand and believe what we are about to tell them. Whether they want to or not, this is the truth which they must be compelled to face, 'for there is no other name under heaven given among men by which we must be saved' (*Acts* 4:12). Such a conviction will fortify us against the contempt of an unbelieving world.

Peter has shown us the way. We begin where our hearers are, then show them how where they are relates to Christ. They may perhaps be lonely, so we take that as our starting-point. But we do not initially promise 'Jesus can cure your loneliness', although that is true. Instead, we show them that their loneliness is merely a symptom of a more profound alienation, their separation from God. We insist that this is their real need and explain how it is possible for them to be reconciled with God and to come to know him as their Father through Christ. Or they may be tense and anxious. We begin there, but not by offering the Son of God as a heavenly sleeping-pill or anti-depressant. Instead, we demonstrate that they have far more reason to be anxious than they realise and that the stress they are experiencing is an indicator of the fearful fact that they are under God's condemnation and heading for hell. But there is a solution. If they trust in Christ, they will be delivered from judgment and experience 'peace with God' (*Rom.* 5:1). Then, and only then, will they be in a position to enjoy 'the peace of God' (*Phil.* 4:7). But this peace must come as a result of salvation, not as a substitute for it.

To return to the medical analogy, it is perfectly proper for a doctor to begin with the symptoms of which the patient complains. But it would be quite wrong for him to become so wrapped up in treating those symptoms that he neglected the underlying disease. People will not listen to sermons which seem to have no connection with life as they know it. Yet preaching which is dominated by this-worldly concerns will be of no ultimate benefit to them. Peter's preaching is both obviously and truly relevant. He starts where people are, then takes them at once to where they need to be. But this is possible only because of the Person who is central in everything he has to say.

8

Christ-centred preaching

We have seen that Peter's sermons, after a brief introduction, always begin with Jesus: they also end in exactly the same way (2:36; 3:26; 4:12; 10:43). Christ is the Alpha and the Omega of all that the apostle has to say. His hearers are directed initially to the Son of God and his last words leave the name of the Saviour echoing in their minds.

But Christ is not only referred to at the beginning and the end of Peter's preaching, he pervades it. This can be shown statistically. In the four sermons under consideration we find specific references to Christ in approximately: thirteen out of twenty-six verses; ten out of fifteen; three out of five; seven out of ten. Out of a total of fifty-six verses, about thirty-three—well over half the words recorded—are about Christ. There can be no mistaking this. He is Peter's great theme.

Is Christ at the centre of our gospel preaching? Is he our supreme subject, at the heart of every message? Do we preach him specifically, or merely talk around and about him? Spurgeon's advice, proved by long and fruitful experience, is still timely: 'I believe that those sermons which are fullest of Christ are the most likely to be blessed to the conversion of the hearers. Let your sermons be full of Christ, from beginning to end crammed full of the gospel. Preach Jesus Christ, brethren, always and everywhere.'[1]

But even more impressive than the number of references to Jesus is the depth and richness of Peter's treatment, for he preaches Christ from at least three perspectives: historically, scripturally, that is from the Old Testament, and doctrinally.

[1] C. H. Spurgeon: *The Soul-Winner* (London: Marshall Brothers, n.d.), p. 108.

[61]

i. The historical Christ

Peter preaches a real-life Jesus, firmly rooted in history. His sermons are not just declarations of faith or appeals to the conscience. They contain detailed accounts of actual incidents in the life and work of the Lord. He provides his hearers with facts, well-remembered and often verifiable. In his Pentecost sermon, we hear of Jesus' home town of Nazareth (2:2), his miracles, wonders and signs (2:22), his crucifixion and death at Gentile hands (2:23) and his resurrection (2:24,30–32). These are not theories or unsupported beliefs. They are historical events.

The Jews who have gathered in Solomon's porch are reminded that it was to Pontius Pilate that they had delivered up God's Servant (3:13) and that they had asked for a murderer to be released in his place (3:14). When preaching in a Gentile household, where the facts about Jesus would not be so well known as among the inhabitants of Jerusalem, Peter is at pains to include extra details. He tells of the ministry of John the Baptist (10:37) and of Jesus' being anointed with the Holy Spirit (10:38), after which he 'went about doing good and healing all who were oppressed by the devil' (10:38). It was on the third day that he was raised from the dead (10:40) and he ate and drank with the disciples after his resurrection (10:41).

New Testament scholarship, particularly in the twentieth century, has mutated into weird forms and wandered into some exceedingly strange blind alleys. Sadly, much of it has been a display of unbelief and misplaced ingenuity rather than a reverent attempt to understand the Scriptures. But nothing has been more ludicrous than the repeated assertion that 'the Jesus of history' must be separated from 'the Christ of faith'. We are told that Jesus of Nazareth probably did exist, but we know practically nothing about him. He is lost in the mists of time, but we do not need him. It matters little whether or not he performed any miracles or even rose from the dead. What is important is 'the Christ of faith', which is no more than the idea of victory over evil, the conviction that love is all and that good must triumph. The apostles, it is alleged, had little interest in 'the Jesus of history'. Their whole focus was upon the heavenly, unseen

Lord of faith and, particularly, the truth which his story represented. We are urged to follow their example.

One need only glance at Peter's sermons, as a representative example of apostolic preaching, to see how absurd this idea is. He knows nothing of any disjunction between history and faith, between Jesus and Christ. They are one and the same. The Christ in whom salvation is offered is the very Jesus who lived, taught, died and rose again. He is neither fantasy nor legend. Again and again Peter stresses the solid historicity of his Master's person and work. He refers, for instance, to the existence of eyewitnesses. The facts about Christ are not unsubstantiated. Both speaker and, occasionally, hearers, have seen these events with their own eyes:

Men of Israel, hear these words: Jesus of Nazareth, a Man attested by God to you by miracles, wonders and signs which God did through Him in your midst, as you yourselves also know . . . This Jesus God has raised up, of which we are all witnesses . . . And we are witnesses of all things which he did both in the land of the Jews and in Jerusalem . . . Him God raised up on the third day, and showed Him openly, not to all the people, but to witnesses chosen before by God, even to us who ate and drank with Him after he arose from the dead (2:22,32; 10:39,40–41).

Even at the end of his life Peter is still insisting upon the historicity of Jesus, reminding his readers that he himself is testifying to what he has seen: 'For we did not follow cunningly devised fables when we made known to you the power and coming of our Lord Jesus Christ, but were eyewitnesses of His majesty' (*2 Pet.* 1:16). The Christ is no cloudy, mythical figure but a real man who accomplished the redemption of his people in time and space. Some years later, Peter's friend John will echo this insistence: 'That which was from the beginning, which we have heard, which we have seen with our eyes, which we have looked upon, and our hands have handled, concerning the Word of life . . . that which we have seen and heard we declare to you . . .' (*1 John* 1:1,3).

A major part of gospel preaching is historical narrative. The events of Christ's life need to be recounted again and again to our hearers, because we are living in a world which is ignorant of the facts on which the message of salvation is based. Few

[63]

have any accurate or detailed knowledge about Jesus. To some he is a vague, unreal being, a kind of Santa Claus. Many use his name as a label to sell their own ideas. He becomes a slogan for whatever cause they are promoting—Jesus the liberator, the revolutionary, the feminist, the pillar of right-wing politics. In a ghastly parody of creation, man is remaking the Son of God in his own image. The resulting versions of Christ may tell us much about their creators, but they shed no light on the Saviour himself. He has become lost in a welter of counterfeits. Most people simply do not know who Jesus of Nazareth is. They have no idea what he did, what he taught or what his life and death mean for us.

So we must tell them. We must take time to teach the events of the Gospel narratives. We should explain where Jesus was born and why it was there, who his mother was and to whom she was married. We should recount the different incidents of his ministry, the names of his disciples, the miracles he performed and the claims which he made for himself. The details of his arrest, trial and crucifixion should be made clear. We need to describe the circumstances of his resurrection and to list the various witnesses who saw him alive after he had been raised from the dead.

Such preaching will not win us a reputation for originality or profound thought. To some it may seem prosaic or childish. But it is vital, for these facts are the soil from which intelligent faith will grow. Breathless exhortations to 'trust Jesus' are all very well, but how much information do people have about the One to whom they are being called to commit their lives? And if they know little about him, what is their response worth? An emotional acceptance of an unknown Lord will produce nothing real or lasting. This is credulity, not saving faith.

Every preacher should want to apply the gospel to his hearers and we shall see later how forcefully Peter did this. But if application is not to degenerate into brainwashing, it must be built on a foundation of truth. The gospel, after all, is 'good news'. What happens when we watch a news broadcast on television? Does the announcer begin by urging us to respond in any particular way? No. Various incidents are reported so that we can understand what has been happening in the world. We may, of course, be moved by these events. We may laugh, shed tears or become angry. But the information comes first.

The analogy is not exact because, unlike a news broadcast, preaching aims at producing a definite response. But we too are to begin with the details of history, what the Son of God became and did for our salvation. These facts have an innate power and persuasiveness. Our primary task as heralds is to make them clear.

ii. The scriptural Christ

The apostles had been eyewitnesses of the life, death and resurrection of Jesus. But in order that their testimony might be corroborated Peter calls on another source to confirm his message. A marked feature of his gospel preaching is the way in which he quotes extensively from the Old Testament. It was his Bible of course, the only written Scripture available to him at this point. But he provides us with a classic example of how to use the Old Testament in evangelistic preaching.

He had already set this expository pattern in his first recorded speech in Acts, where he developed the theme of choosing an apostolic successor to Judas, by way of reference to Psalms 69 and 109 (*Acts* 1:20,21). He now continues by showing how Christ was foretold in the Old Testament. On the day of Pentecost he quotes from Joel 2 (*Acts* 2:16–21) and Psalms 16 (*Acts* 2:25–28) and 110 (*Acts* 2:34,35). The sermon in Solomon's porch has references to Deuteronomy 18 (*Acts* 3:22,23), and his address to the Sanhedrin concludes with a searching application of Psalm 118 (*Acts* 4:11).

Why does Peter make so many citations from the Hebrew Scriptures? It is because he wants to establish that God had planned and foretold the saving work of Christ long before it happened. This would be a powerful argument with his Jewish hearers, committed as they were to the Old Testament as the oracles of God. The message of the gospel was not a suspect revelation from an alien source. It was there, plain to see, in their synagogue scrolls. 'This is what was spoken' (2:16) is his theme. The Old Testament prophesies Christ and its predictions have now come to pass: 'Those things which God foretold by the mouth of all His prophets, that the Christ

[65]

would suffer, he has thus fulfilled' (3:18); 'All the prophets, from Samuel and those who follow, as many as have spoken, have also foretold these things' (3:24); 'To Him all the prophets witness' (10:43).

Peter is thoroughly familiar with the Old Testament. This was to be expected from a pious Jew, trained from childhood to memorise the Scriptures. But what is striking is that, even at this early stage of the church's post-resurrection history, he has meditated deeply on the relationship between the prophecies and Christ. His thinking was guided by the risen Lord when he was seen by the apostles over a period of forty days, 'speaking of the things pertaining to the kingdom of God' (*Acts* 1:3). At the heart of Jesus' teaching was his own identity and work as expounded in the Hebrew Scriptures: 'Then He said to them, "These are the words which I spoke to you while I was still with you, that all things must be fulfilled which were written in the law of Moses and the Prophets and the Psalms concerning Me." And He opened their understanding, that they might comprehend the Scriptures' (*Luke* 24:44,45).

This is why Peter has already developed a profound christological interpretation of the Old Testament. The ancient jewels of revelation glow with a lustre which is altogether new. He sees Jesus everywhere. Law and covenant, psalms and prophets—all are radiant with the glory of God's Son. This Galilean fisherman handles Scripture in such a masterly way that the experts of the Sanhedrin are confounded before him.

Peter lived in days of directly-given revelation. He saw Jesus with his own eyes. One of the 'divided tongues, as of fire' sat upon him, so that he was filled with the Holy Spirit and proclaimed the wonderful works of God in a language he had never learned (2:3,4,11). He himself performed miracles of healing (3:6–8; 9:34,40) and was the instrument through whom two liars were struck down dead (5:1–11). He had a vision (10:8–16) and was twice delivered from prison by an angel of the Lord (5:19; 12:7–10). Yet what excites this privileged believer in the midst of such wonders? The Bible! This is because it is the written Word of God and it witnesses to his Saviour. Even when reflecting upon that supreme moment on the Mount of Transfiguration, when he and his friends were eyewitnesses of Christ's majesty (*2 Pet.* 1:16), and heard the voice of God the Father from the excellent glory, he is compelled to remind his readers at once of a superior testimony: 'We also have the prophetic word made more sure, which you do well to heed as a light that shines in a dark place . . .' (*2 Pet.* 1:19).

That light of written revelation shines more brightly for us than it did for Peter, because our Scriptures are more extensive than his. In the New Testament we have the inspired record of the life and ministry of the Saviour. The Gospels tell us what God did in Christ and the epistles provide an authoritative interpretation of the meaning of those redemptive events. It is inevitable, then, that much of our evangelistic preaching will be based on the New Testament, for it contains the full and final disclosure of salvation. But we would lose a great deal if we were to neglect the Old Testament in our proclamation of the gospel.

Yet it is overlooked all too often. This may be due to a false theology which divides the activity of God into various epochs, self-contained and independent of each other. It is claimed that God, in the gospel age, operates on principles entirely different from those which obtained in the Old Testament. There is no continuity of purpose. Whereas previously all was law with no grace, now all is grace with no law. This being so, the Old Testament, from an obsolete dispensation, can have little to say about the message of salvation.

Sections of the church have been infected by what is misleadingly called 'liberal' theology. This mind-set, inspired by the theory of evolution, sees the Old Testament as a primitive book, presenting a bloodthirsty, vengeful Jehovah. It is only in the more enlightened New Testament, we are told, that we find a God of love, the father of our Lord Jesus Christ. To preach the gospel from the Old Testament would be impossible, for it would mark a regression to an age of superstition and cruelty.

Even in Reformed circles there is a growing reluctance to use the Old Testament in evangelism. The ablest biblical interpreters have always emphasised the importance of approaching passages from the viewpoint of the writer and his primary audience. We cannot decide what the text means for us today until we understand what it meant to those to and through whom it was originally given. This is true and such a discipline will keep us from far-fetched allegorising and a spiritualising which is no more than reading into Scripture our own ideas. But this method of grammatico-historical exegesis, sound though it may be, is in danger of going too far and toppling over into error. It is failing to recognise that there is a valid and essential spiritualising of Scripture. It is coming too close to treating the Word of God like any ordinary book. Some preachers are imprisoned by it as in a straitjacket, afraid of bringing any more from an Old Testament passage than a few arid reflections on the development of the history of redemption to that point.

The apostles however have no inhibitions about finding and preaching Christ throughout the Old Testament. Paul, for example, sees him in the singular 'Seed' promised to Abraham (*Gal.* 3:16) and in the water-producing rock in the wilderness (*1 Cor.* 10:4). Peter himself implies that we cannot limit the meaning of a passage to what was understood by the original writers, who could not always comprehend the revelation they had received (*1 Pet.* 1:10–12). His frequent citations of the Old Testament in his gospel preaching encourage us to use it in the same way.

How persuasive it will be when we show our hearers the accuracy with which Jesus and his sufferings were foretold centuries before he came to earth! As we explain to them the amazing detail of the prophecies, their faith will be awakened and they will come to see that this message must be from God. How enlightening are the sacrifices, ceremonies and types recorded in the books of Moses! The spotless lamb, the holy of holies, the sprinkling of blood—all speak vividly of salvation. Is our preaching dull? Do people understand what we are saying? These visual aids have a colour and immediacy which will reach many who would be left cold by concepts and abstractions. How thrilling are the accounts of God rescuing his people from their enemies in Egypt, Canaan and Babylon and how compellingly they illustrate the greater deliverance from the power of Satan!

Should we neglect the Old Testament because we have the New? Never! In fact, the reverse is the case. It is precisely because Christ and his salvation have been revealed that we should preach from the Old Testament all the more, since it is only now that it can be understood properly. Andrew Bonar makes this point by quoting from a letter written by his friend, Robert Murray M'Cheyne:

Suppose that one to whom you were a stranger was wrapt in a thick veil, so that you could not discern his features; still, if the lineaments were pointed out to you through the folds, you could form some idea of the beauty and form of the veiled one. But suppose that one whom you know and love—whose features you have often studied face to face—were to be veiled up in this way, how easily you would discern the features and form of this beloved one! Just so the Jews looked upon a veiled Saviour, whom they had never seen unveiled. We, under the New Testament, look upon an unveiled Saviour; and, going back to the Old, we can see far better than the Jews could, the features and form of Jesus the Beloved, under that veil.[1]

iii. The doctrinal Christ

The apostle Paul is generally recognised as one of the most brilliant intellects in history. His expositions of Christian doctrine are incomparable in their scope and insight. John, the beloved disciple, was nicknamed 'the theologian' by the early church. His many-layered meditations on the Son of God are among the most profound in Scripture. But Peter? Surely here is a down-to-earth, straightforward figure, with little aptitude for complex thought. His famous statement about Paul's epistles, 'in which are some things hard to understand' (*2 Pet.* 3:16) has itself been widely misinterpreted. Peter is not saying that he cannot understand the writings of his fellow-apostle. The remainder of the verse makes it clear that he is referring to 'those who are untaught and unstable', who 'twist to their own destruction' Paul's teaching, 'as they do also the rest of the Scriptures'. But the damage has been done. Peter's reputation is that of a simple man of action, an enthusiastic practical evangelist. We expect him to be vigorous and earnest, but not particularly deep. If this has been our view, we are mistaken.

Peter is a considerable theologian in his own right, but he is

[1] Andrew Bonar, *Leviticus* (Banner of Truth Trust, 1966), pp. 8–9.

a theologian who preaches theology to the unconverted. The reports of his sermons in Acts are no more than summaries, brief outlines of his main emphases. The themes he mentions would have been expanded substantially in preaching. But they are enough to show us that his evangelistic messages were thoroughly doctrinal.

His sermon on the day of Pentecost presents Jesus as Messiah (2:36), ever-living Lord (2:21,34–36), the Holy One of God (2:27), the King of David's line (2:29–32) and the giver of the Holy Spirit (2:33). He preaches to the crowd in Solomon's porch about the Suffering Servant (3:13,26), the Holy and Just One (3:14), the Prince of life (3:15), the promised Prophet like Moses (3:22–24) and the seed of Abraham (3:25–26). The Jewish religious leaders are told about the rejected stone which has now become the chief corner-stone (4:11) and that Jesus of Nazareth is the only Saviour under heaven (4:12). Peter preaches to the Gentiles in the home of Cornelius that Jesus Christ is Lord of all (10:36), Judge of the living and the dead (10:42). The reference to Christ's death 'by hanging on a tree' (10:39) contains the whole doctrine of the substitutionary atonement. His choice of 'tree' instead of 'cross', repeated in 1 Peter 2:24, is governed by his understanding, shared by Paul (*Gal.* 3:10–13), that, at Calvary, Christ took the place of the cursed lawbreaker of Deuteronomy 21:22–23.

What a mighty weight of doctrine! Each of the above references could in itself form the subject of a book. They are packed with meaning, taking us deep into the immensities of God's revelation of his Son. This Saviour whom Peter preaches is awesome in his person and work, his sufferings and glory.

His theological insight extends beyond the person of Christ to such topics as God's predestinating purpose and the doctrine of the last things. Although the crucifixion was a wicked act, it was nevertheless within the sovereign plan of the Almighty. Behind the 'lawless hands' is the comforting reality that Jesus was 'delivered by the determined counsel and foreknowledge of God' (2:23). The outpouring of the Spirit is in fulfilment of an Old Testament prophecy, but Peter significantly alters Joel's wording. 'And it shall come to pass afterward' (*Joel* 2:28) becomes 'and it shall come to pass in the last days' (2:17). The preacher understands that he and his hearers are now in 'the last days', since Christ, by his death and resurrection, has ushered in the final stage of God's programme of redemption. That redemption has implications for the whole creation, not just for individuals, because Jesus at his second coming will bring 'the times of restoration of all things' (3:21).

As a theologian, Peter has neither the range nor the depth of Paul. But the Galilean fisherman preaches a Saviour of infinite majesty. Here is someone before whom we feel compelled to bow down and worship. In the words of Herman Ridderbos, 'Peter is certainly the first in his preaching. Others will join him and the words of Peter will develop in their words. But they will never exceed Peter in the gloriousness of his witness concerning Jesus Christ.'[1]

The implication of this for our preaching is clear. We must preach Christ theologically. We must give our lives to exploring the doctrines of the person and work of the Son of God and to making these plain to our hearers. This is just as true when we are preaching the gospel as when we are expounding God's Word to believers. When Peter stands up to evangelize, he takes his listeners into the profundities of the theology of the Saviour. They hear massive truths, designed to enlighten their minds and pierce their consciences.

How different is so much of the evangelism of today! Any suggestion that gospel preaching should be theological would be greeted with horror. It would be considered a recipe for failure, a sure way of confusing and alienating those whom we want to reach. Modern evangelism aims at being entertaining. Polished musical items are succeeded by personal testimonies from the famous or those whose experience is spectacular. The whole programme is fast-moving. Preaching is anecdotal, brief, leavened by humour. Christ is proclaimed, but often in the shallowest way. He is a friend, a 'need-meeter', an exciting example. The portrait painted is unutterably feeble. This attenuated figure can evoke no awe; no fear; no intense,

---

[1] H. N. Ridderbos, *The Speeches of Peter in the Acts of the Apostles* (Tyndale Press, 1962), p. 27

overwhelming gratitude and love. Sinners are not enabled to marvel at his majesty. There is little sense of the amazing grace of God the Father in giving such a glorious Son to such dreadful punishment for creatures so unworthy. The declared aim is to make the gospel easy for unbelievers to understand. But a two-dimensional, cardboard Christ, supported by folksy stories and a few trite exhortations is not worth understanding.

Even those of us who seek to exercise a responsible, biblical ministry may attempt too little in our gospel preaching. We may be reluctant to plunge into the doctrines. We may confuse what is childishly simplistic with what is childlike and simple. We may cheat our listeners by giving them too little substance. The Christ we preach may be a lesser figure than the Christ we know. If so, we should learn from Peter's example.

God's truth can be trusted. We do not need to water it down in order to make it palatable. We are to preach Christ in the fullness of his being and grace. We are to hold nothing back which God has revealed. We should not ask 'How little do people need to know in order to be saved?' and then aim at this minimum. Instead it should be our goal to tell as much about Jesus Christ as we possibly can. The Holy Spirit will bless such faithful teaching. He will use the doctrines of his Word to convict and convert those destined for salvation. God saves through theology.

Jesus said, 'I, if I am lifted up from the earth, will draw all peoples to Myself' (*John* 12:32). He was lifted up on the cross. Now it is our privilege to lift him up in preaching. Our subject is inexhaustible, effective, glorious. What a challenge for a life's ministry!

9

Bold preaching

When God himself chooses to put on record a particular characteristic of Peter's preaching, we may be sure that it is important. One of its outstanding qualities, mentioned several times in the Book of Acts, is boldness. Peter intended to preach in this way: 'Men and brethren, let me speak freely (lit. boldly) to you of the patriarch David. . .' (2:29). His hearers observed it: 'Now when they saw the boldness of Peter and John, and perceived that they were uneducated and untrained men, they marvelled' (4:13). Believers sought it in prayer for their leaders: 'Now, Lord, look on their threats, and grant to Your servants that with all boldness they may speak Your word' (4:29). God answered this prayer abundantly, not just for Peter, when 'they were all filled with the Holy Spirit, and they spoke the word of God with boldness' (4:31). What does it mean to preach boldly?

The Greek word for boldness is *parresia* and it has a wide range of uses. It literally means 'saying everything', and in classical Greek it referred to the right of every citizen in a democracy to speak out frankly. All Athenians, for example, had equal status before the law. When the city assembly met, no-one needed to be intimidated into silence. Every member had the privilege of stating his opinions openly. He did not need to conceal his views or refrain from making suggestions. He had *parresia*—bold, clear, uninhibited speech.

The New Testament uses the word with varying nuances, which require differing translations. In the Gospels it often means 'plainly'. After Peter had confessed that Jesus was the Messiah, his Master began to explain with new clarity the facts of his rejection, death and resurrection. 'He spoke this word openly' (*Mark* 8:32). When the disciples mistakenly thought that Jesus was speaking about a sleeping Lazarus, 'Jesus said to them plainly, Lazarus is dead' (*John* 11:14). Sometimes the reference is to what is done in public, without concealment. When Jesus was questioned by the high priest about his teaching, he answered, 'I spoke openly to the world. I always taught in synagogues and in the temple, where the Jews always meet, and in secret I have said nothing. Ask those who have heard me what I said to them. Indeed they know what I said' (*John* 18:20–21).

In the epistles of Hebrews and 1 John, *parresia* is a keynote of new covenant spirituality, referring to a joyful confidence before God. We are encouraged to 'come boldly to the throne of grace . . . having boldness to enter the Holiest by the blood of Jesus' (*Heb.* 4:16; 10:19). John urges us to 'abide in Him, that, when He appears, we may have confidence and not be ashamed before Him at His coming' (*1 John* 2:28).

Boldness in Acts, and in some of Paul's writings, contains all these ideas of clarity, openness and confidence. But added to them is the concept of courage before men. This results from our acceptance by God. Since Christ Jesus is our Lord 'in whom we have boldness and access with confidence through faith in Him' (*Eph.* 3:12), we need not be intimidated by anyone else. The bold speaker, especially when facing those who are powerful or hostile, is fearless in what he says. He is not shackled in any way. He does not select his words with extreme care to avoid any possibility of offence. Gripped by a truth which he is passionately concerned to convey, he pours his whole being into telling his hearers what they need to know. Paul could remind the Thessalonians, 'We were bold in our God to speak to you the gospel of God in much conflict . . . as we have been approved by God to be entrusted with the gospel, even so we speak, not as pleasing men, but God who tests our hearts' (*1 Thess.* 2:2,4). It is in this sense of courageous speech that Peter was a bold preacher.

His boldness is seen most clearly in the remarkably direct way in which he applies the truth to his audience. Again and again he plunges the sword of the Spirit up to the hilt in the consciences of his hearers. The Pentecost crowds are left in no doubt as to where the main responsibility for the murder of Jesus lies: 'Men of Israel, hear these words: Jesus of Nazareth, a Man attested by God to you by miracles, wonders and signs which God did through Him in your midst, as you yourselves also know, Him . . . you have taken by lawless hands, have crucified and put to death' (2:22,23).

We are sometimes told that a preacher should avoid the second person plural and restrict himself to the first person—the 'gracious we' instead of the 'condemnatory you'. Peter has no such inhibitions. In almost every phrase of his application comes the pointed 'you'. We can see his stabbing finger and flashing eyes and hear the hiss of indrawn breath from listeners so personally identified. In case they have missed the point, the preacher includes one more piercing thrust in his closing statement: 'Therefore let all the house of Israel know assuredly that God has made this Jesus, whom you crucified, both Lord and Christ' (2:36).

But perhaps this was Peter on a bad day! Had he got out of bed on the wrong side that morning? Is this sermon a sour exception, this pointed application uncharacteristic? Not at all. His second evangelistic message is, if anything, even more direct: 'The God of Abraham, Isaac, and Jacob, the God of our fathers, glorified His Servant Jesus, whom you delivered up and denied in the presence of Pilate, when he was determined to let Him go. But you denied the Holy One and the Just, and asked for a murderer to be granted to you, and killed the Prince of life' (3:13–15).

This is a devastating indictment. The Roman governor had no wish to punish Jesus and did all he could to have him released. But it was Christ's own people, the children of the covenant, who denied Israel's Messiah and insisted that the Gentiles crucify him. Blessed above all others, they trampled on their privileges and spurned the Saviour whom God had sent to them. How inexcusable their sin!

When Peter addresses the Sanhedrin, he might be forgiven for moderating his language. These are, after all, the leaders of his nation, experts in the law of God. If displeased, they have the power to have him put to death. Surely now, if ever, is the time to be tactfully indirect. Not in any way! 'Let it be known to you all . . . that by the name of Jesus Christ of Nazareth, whom you crucified, whom God raised from the dead, by Him this man stands here before you whole' (4:10). Peter even chooses to sharpen an Old Testament quotation. Citing Psalm 118:22—'The stone which the builders rejected has become the cornerstone'—he alters 'the builders' to 'This is the stone which was rejected by you builders' (4:11). He is not changing the meaning of Scripture, because he understands that this is the climactic fulfilment of the prophecy. The Jewish leaders are 'the builders' foretold by the Psalmist and it is quite legitimate to address them as 'you'. But his interest is not so much in Old Testament interpretation as in convicting his hearers of their sin.

Yet he wants to persuade them also that God is offering mercy in Christ to each one of them. He is direct not only in preaching sin but in preaching grace. People are guilty, but Christ is a mighty Saviour. So the promises and encouragements of the gospel are impressed as urgently upon those who hear as are the threats and warnings: 'Repent, and let every one of you be baptized in the name of Jesus Christ for the remission of sins; and you shall receive the gift of the Holy Spirit. For the promise is to you and to your children' (2:38,39). Or again, 'Yet now, brethren, I know that you did it in ignorance . . .Repent therefore and be converted, that your sins may be blotted out . . . You are the sons of the prophets, and of the covenant which God made with our fathers . . . To you first, God, having raised up His Servant Jesus, sent Him to bless you, in turning away every one of you from your iniquities' (3:17,19,24–26). The tone is boldly personal. Peter is not hiding behind generalities, but is addressing each individual in the most urgent and intimate way.

Are there men today who preach so directly? The last thirty-five years have seen the re-publication of the best theological and devotional writings of the previous four and a half centuries. Increasing numbers of conservative biblical scholars are at work and gifted contemporary authors are emerging. These rich literary resources have led to, and been accompanied by, a marked improvement in the quality of training offered for the ministry. The net result has been to produce some very talented expositors of Scripture. While many are doubtless born to bloom unseen in remote churches, others enjoy a wide sphere of influence. Their theology is orthodox, their interpretations responsible and accurate, their ability to arrange and present their material outstanding. The sermons they preach are polished and interesting. We listen to them with pleasure and thank God for them. What a blessing it is to have ministers so competent in explaining the meaning of the Bible!

But something is missing. There is little of what the Puritans called 'close dealing'. The preacher expounds a passage and shows its general relevance to his hearers. So far, so good. But there he stops. He hopes that people will make their own application and urges them to do so. He has indicated what the text means and how it should be applied. But he does not seek to drive it home to their consciences. He does not grapple them to himself and passionately press the truth upon them. He does not brush aside the polite conventions and dare to speak to them soul to soul, with a transparent and challenging urgency. There are few piercing questions, designed to linger in their memories. Indeed, such directness is frowned on. It is considered a breach of good manners to be too insistent, in poor taste, almost a usurping of the convicting work of the Holy Spirit. Men and women must make up their own minds. After all, we are not foot-in-the-door salesmen.

Now it is certainly dangerous to try to apply God's Word to other people. Such application can all too easily degenerate into abuse. We can violate the integrity of the human personality by emotional blackmail, or by trampling on delicate sensibilities. The preacher can turn into a bully. A man may think that he is speaking forcefully when he is simply spewing out the bile of his own ill-nature. It is so very hard to be direct and, at the same time, gentle and loving.

Our consciousness of indwelling sin also inhibits us. How do we urge upon others an obedience which we render so imperfectly ourselves? Are we not coming perilously close to deserving our Lord's words: 'How can you say to your brother, Let me remove the speck out of your eye; and look, a plank is in your own eye? Hypocrite! First remove the plank from your own eye' (*Matt.* 7:4,5)?

Yet, difficult or not, it must be done. Peter's ministry proves

that the gospel preacher must address listeners very personally. If he hopes to bring them to salvation, he must first
impress upon them their lostness. He must seek to make them
feel the shame and pain of sin. He must hammer home the
nails of conviction. In the denomination in which I serve one
of the questions put to every minister at ordination is: 'Do you
promise, through grace . . . in preaching, not to be satisfied
with a general statement of doctrine, but to be careful to
speak to the conscience in a direct and searching manner?'

This is where boldness is needed. An especially striking
example of such boldness is the charge brought by Peter
when he reminds the crowd of 'Jesus, whom you delivered up
and denied in the presence of Pilate . . . you denied the Holy
One' (3:13,14). The verb 'denied' grates on the ear. Were
they the only ones to deny the Saviour? Is their denial not
overshadowed by another one, far more public and inexcusable? Has Peter forgotten so soon the courtyard of the high
priest's house and the disciple who denied his Master? He
had been warned by Christ. He had made a vehement
promise: 'If I have to die with you, I will not deny you'
(*Mark* 14:31). But he had denied him, three times, with
curses. Yet he now has the nerve to stand up and accuse
other people of denying Jesus! Surely, if ever, here is a case for
the first person plural, a repentant 'we denied the Holy One'!

Yet this would be to misunderstand the very purpose of
preaching the gospel. It is not to demonstrate the humility of
the preacher. Peter is not being hypocritical. He is not
overlooking his own sin or pretending that he is better than
he really is. He needs no convincing of his personal unworthiness. The tragedy of Judas is a painful recent memory. They
had been colleagues, fellow-disciples. One is now in a suicide's
grave, the other is a preacher and only the grace of God
has made the difference. In the proper context, Peter will
acknowledge his own wrongdoing. When he provides Mark
with the information on which the second Gospel is based, he
will detail his disobedience and failures, so that the record will
stand for ever of what he was.

But that is of no relevance now. The great issue is the
spiritual state of those to whom he is speaking. They are lost
and he has the only message which can save them. It is his

duty to deliver it as forcefully as he can, forgetting about himself and thinking of nothing but how to bring home to these poor sinners their need of Christ.

Shall we hesitate to apply the gospel because of our own unworthiness? Shall we tone down our preaching for fear of being thought arrogant or holier-than-thou? Is this not pride masquerading as humility? As we preach, only one thing matters—that the message of salvation should be brought home to those who hear us. Nothing can be allowed to blunt the impact of what we are saying, certainly not any self-centred desire to be liked.

Of course we must search our own hearts. We must feel keenly the pain of our sinfulness. But the place for this is in secret, not in the pulpit. Deep repentance and humiliation of soul, if they are genuine, will make us meek and gentle. It should be obvious from our demeanour whether or not we place ourselves on a pedestal. But it is a tragic mistake to preach timidly because we are imperfect. Christ, our theme, is perfect. Let us proclaim him without constraint.

For this, we pray for a holy boldness. It seems to be a constant need of preachers. Paul asked the Ephesians to intercede for him 'that utterance may be given to me, that I may open my mouth boldly, to make known the mystery of the gospel, that I may speak boldly, as I ought to speak' (*Eph.* 6:19,20). Secured through prayer, its immediate parents are a passion for the salvation of the lost and a persuasion that the gospel is true. Paul is a bold preacher because he is convinced that the gospel and its ministry are far superior to the law and the ministry of Moses: 'Therefore, since we have such hope, we use great boldness of speech' (*2 Cor.* 3:12). Charles Hodge comments:

If Paul's experience of the truth and excellence of the gospel led him to declare it without reserve, a similar experience will produce a similar openness and boldness in other ministers of the gospel. This indeed is one of the glories of Christianity . . .If a man in a church has the conviction that the gospel is of God, that it is unspeakably glorious, adapted to all and needed by all in order to salvation, then the word will be preached openly and without reserve.[1]

[1] Charles Hodge, *First & Second Corinthians* (Banner of Truth Trust, 1974), pp. 440–1.

Boldness is a spiritual grace and it is easy to counterfeit, but the differences between a natural and a godly boldness are profound. In the words of Charles Bridges:

It is not an affected faithfulness, that makes a merit of provoking hostility to the truth—not a presumptuous rashness, that utters the holy oracles without premeditation of what is most fitting to be said, or most likely to be effective. But it is a spiritual, holy principle, combined with meekness, humility, and love, and with deep consciousness of our own weakness and infirmities.[1]

There is so much in the world to intimidate us. Our culture is hostile to authority and dogmatism. Tolerance is the supreme virtue and any claim to absolute truth will offend. It is not easy to tell people we like, and in some respects admire, that their way of life is wrong and that they are headed for hell. These pressures and others militate against boldness in preaching and many men have succumbed.

But we need to seek this grace from the Lord. We should throw off innate timidity and show our hearers that we really mean what we say and that, as was reported of Robert Murray M'Cheyne, we are 'dying' to have them converted. Martyn Lloyd-Jones' comments are typically perceptive:

We are all so diplomatic, we are all so concerned about dignity, we are all so concerned about being 'scholarly' and not causing offence; we are all so afraid of fanaticism! We are so afraid of being too extreme, of being too emphatic! . . . Endless qualifications make the message indefinite and uncertain . . . What is said at the beginning is often taken back at the end, and you do not know where you are . . . (Paul says) Pray that I may have strength to preach it without qualifications, without fear. Take from me any desire to be considered learned. Pray that I may preach the gospel boldly, not elegantly, that I may preach it in truth, not in a manner that appeals to the public palate. And that I may never be a man-pleaser, or afraid to face the scorn and the abuse of men.[2]

[1] Charles Bridges, *The Christian Ministry* (Banner of Truth Trust, 1967), p. 298.
[2] D. Martyn Lloyd-Jones, *The Christian Soldier: An Exposition of Ephesians 6:10–20* (Banner of Truth Trust, 1977), pp. 360–1.

Except that our boldness will be rewarded with more than scorn and abuse. For Peter's boldness was blessed, in that 'when they heard this, they were cut to the heart, and said to Peter and the rest of the apostles, "Men and brethren, what shall we do?"' (2:37). If we preach with similar directness, we too may anticipate that there will be many saved through our preaching, eager to thank God for our loving courage.

10

Preaching the demands of grace

Peter was not afraid of being called a negative preacher. As we have studied his sermons, we have seen him taking pains to identify and condemn sin. He has brought home to his hearers in the most pointed way their wickedness and guilt. Before any offer of mercy has come the stark declaration that they have broken the commandments of God. There is a sternness, almost a fierceness, about him. One of his aims is to wound, to break, to convict. He preaches the holy law of God in its majesty and terror.

But his preaching is more than law. He is not standing up merely to denounce, for his chief purpose is altogether positive—the salvation of those who are listening to him. Peter loves to end his sermons with a grace-note. In all the messages we are considering, he closes by declaring God's provision of salvation for all who will trust in his Son. Forgiveness in Christ is the climax towards which he always moves.

The audience on the day of Pentecost have been convicted of their sin in crucifying Jesus: 'Now when they heard this, they were cut to the heart, and said to Peter and the rest of the apostles, Men and brethren, what shall we do?' (2:37). But their cry of anguished fear is answered by a promise of incredible grace: 'Repent, and let every one of you be baptized in the name of Jesus Christ for the remission of sins; and you shall receive the gift of the Holy Spirit' (2:38). What an amazing statement! They were responsible for the death of Christ and yet their sins may be forgiven. They murdered God's Son and he is offering them his Spirit.

Such a promise is repeated in every sermon. The Jews have

[82]

killed the Prince of life, but 'To you first, God, having raised up His Servant Jesus, sent Him to bless you, in turning away every one of you from your iniquities' (3:26). The rulers and elders of Israel have rejected Jesus Christ, the only hope of mankind, and are told, 'Nor is there salvation in any other, for there is no other name under heaven given among men by which we must be saved' (4:12). That is a piece of information which is utterly devastating. Can it be that they have put to death their only hope? No, because God has raised the crucified One from the dead and his name is now being proclaimed to them as Saviour. In spite of their guilt, they may still be delivered. Cornelius and his Gentile friends may have wondered if, as those outside the historic covenant people, they could ever be sure of mercy, but the good news of the gospel is that 'through His name, whoever believes in Him will receive remission of sins' (10:43).

These words can lie inertly on the page and it is all too easy to miss the wonder of what Peter is saying. But think about it! Human beings, condemned to death, are being offered a new beginning. If they will come to Christ, God will forgive all their sins and receive them as his beloved children. Salvation in its fullness will be theirs. A new and glorious existence will open up before them. For the first time they will know peace, security, a purpose for life and a certain hope beyond it. What a thrilling prospect!

Peter, moreover, makes this offer to every single one of his hearers. He is, of course, well aware that only those will come to Christ who are irresistibly summoned by God the Spirit, 'For the promise is to you and to your children, and to all who are afar off, as many as the Lord our God will call' (2:39). But this does not inhibit him in any way from promising mercy in the most general terms: 'Repent, and let every one of you be baptized in the name of Jesus Christ for the remission of sins; and you shall receive the gift of the Holy Spirit' (2:38); 'God, having raised up His Servant Jesus, sent Him to bless you, in turning away every one of you from your iniquities' (3:26); 'through His name, whoever believes in Him will receive remission of sins' (10:43). God's generosity is staggering. Absolutely no-one who hears the gospel need feel excluded. No-one can say, 'This is not for me'. 'Every one of you—every one of you—whoever'—all, without exception, should come to Christ. He offers to save them and is willing to receive them. Only those who exclude themselves are excluded.

Here is the warm-hearted generosity of true gospel preaching. It brings good news—the best—to all who will believe. It is a message to be delivered and received with exultant joy. With every fibre of his being, the preacher is to emphasise the grace of God in his Son. There is an unearthly extravagance about the magnificence and freeness of the offer of salvation in Christ.

But do we speak like this? Do we give the impression of something overwhelmingly great and glorious? Is it not often the case that our preaching of Christ is heavily qualified, cautious, almost grudging? We have a good deal to say about effort and duty. We do not seem to be sure if what we say applies to everyone. More stress is laid on what sinners must do than on what God has done. Too many preach the gospel with a frown instead of a smile, clenched fists instead of open arms.

Why is this so? Some may not be convinced that the offer of salvation should be made to everyone. These Christians know that, before the world was made, God chose a people to be his and that those persons alone will be saved. They are the elect for whom Christ died and in whom the Spirit will work. They know also that unconverted men and women cannot by themselves come to Christ. Dead in their sins, they simply do not have the ability to repent and believe. In the light of these facts, some think it illogical to offer the Saviour freely to all. But we dare not allow the straitjacket of our puny logic to cramp the marvellous freeness of the gospel. In our preaching, we should not feel compelled to be less generous or more apparently logical than the apostle. As Peter makes plain, Jesus Christ is to be offered as Saviour to all who hear us and this offer is genuine, to be made with all our hearts.

Perhaps the preacher is afraid that his hearers may try to take advantage of God. People are naturally dishonest and selfish. Is it safe to offer salvation to them on such exceedingly generous terms as those laid down in the Bible? Will they not misunderstand or abuse such kindness? Is there not a real danger of their merely pretending to believe in Christ? Might it not therefore be wiser to hedge the gospel round with a few conditions just to keep them on the straight and narrow?

This has been the well-meaning but disastrous reasoning of many ever since 'certain men came down from Judea and taught the brethren, "Unless you are circumcised according to the custom of Moses, you cannot be saved"' (15:1). We could call it 'Christ plus'. Christ alone is not enough for salvation. Something must be added. The plus may be a set of rules, a ritual, an experience or a certain standard of behaviour. It matters little. For the end result is always the same — the destruction of the gospel.

The Lord knows what he is doing! Whenever we try to be wiser than he, we invariably destroy what we intend to protect. We need to throw aside all hesitancy and preach the gospel exactly as he has revealed it. 'Believe on the Lord Jesus Christ, and you will be saved, you and your household' (16:31). No 'ifs' or 'buts', no escape clauses for the preacher or conditions for the hearer. Christ will save every person who trusts in him — full stop! God's grace is truly free.

But it is not cheap. Indeed the very extent of the divine kindness is itself challenging. A message like this demands a response. We can hardly react to such an amazingly generous gift with an indifferent shrug of the shoulders, because the freeness of the offer imposes an obligation on those to whom it is made. So all Peter's sermons end with a challenge which is clear and specific. His listeners have a decision to make. They must consciously obey or reject the message and the preacher allows them no avenue of escape, no comfortable neutral option. He leaves them in no doubt that there is something which they are being called to do, then and there.

What is it? That also is made plain: 'Repent and be baptized in the name of Jesus Christ' (2:38); 'repent and be converted' (3:19); 'believe in Him' (10:43). They are to turn decisively from their sin and humble themselves by trusting, as Saviour, the one whom they had previously despised. They are to do so immediately. To delay would be an insult to the God who is extending to them such an outstanding offer of mercy. 'Come to Christ now,' exhorts Peter. 'Do not let another moment pass before you cry to him for salvation. Do not leave this place until you have closed with Jesus.' The demand is simple but compelling.

Have we lost this sense of urgency and immediacy, this pressing summons to make at once the most important of life's decisions? Do we plead with our hearers to receive the Saviour even as we speak? Do we pray, before, during and after preaching, that people will be converted that very day? Is it not all too often the case that our evangelistic appeal is directed towards an uncertain future? We ask our hearers to trust in Christ somehow and at some indefinite time. When and how is left up to them.

One of the many stories about C. H. Spurgeon tells how he listened with mounting exasperation to someone leading in public prayer. The good man who was praying dwelt at inordinate length on the various attributes of God, the unworthiness of the people gathered and the discouraging nature of the times in which they lived. As he meandered on without making one request or offering a single intercession, Spurgeon's impatience increased until he could contain himself no longer. 'Brother', he interrupted, 'ask Him for something!' People can feel like saying that when listening to preaching. All too often it asks nothing definite from them. The sermon proceeds on its stately course, interesting or dull as the case may be, and then comes to a stop. But what response are they meant to make to the Word of God? They are never told. The truth is proclaimed and then left hanging in the air. If someone wanted to respond, they would not know how. Perhaps at times they long to say, 'Brother, ask us for something! What are we to do? Show us how to put God's Word into practice'. No-one ever needed to say that after Peter had finished speaking.

Why are some preachers reluctant to demand an immediate response to their message? They may be overreacting against a type of ministry which gives people the impression that the question of salvation is entirely in their own hands. This mentality is called 'decisionism', because it sees the human decision as the all-important factor. God, in sending his Son to the cross, has done all that he can. Now it is up to the individual. Will he or she decide to follow Christ? Everything hinges on whether or not they can be persuaded and all the efforts of the preacher are focused on moving the sinner's will.

Some are rightly repelled by this unbiblical approach and eager to maintain that 'salvation is of the Lord' (*Jon.* 2:9). They know that the crucial element in the conversion of any individual is the regenerating work of the Holy Spirit. Unless he gives new life, no-one can or will repent and believe. So far, so good. But at this point can come the imbalance. Reluctant to suggest in any way that man can claim some of the credit for his own salvation, they lean too far in the other direction and come close to ignoring the gospel demand altogether. Anxious not to fall into one error, they go to the other extreme and leave their hearers unaware of what God is telling them to do. Peter will have none of such timidity. 'Here is what God expects from you', he tells his audience. 'Repent now. Believe now. This is your duty.'

Sometimes a hesitation to challenge our hearers to an instant response springs from a less worthy source—a lack of confidence in the power of the gospel. We assume that little or nothing will happen as a result of our preaching. In our heart of hearts we do not expect to see conversions. Long, disappointing experience has taught us not to hope for too much. In all probability, no-one will come to faith.

We cannot admit this openly, however, because the purpose of preaching the gospel is to bring sinners to Christ. If we do not think that they will come, why preach? So we reshape our goals in order to maintain a facade of optimism. If we were to call people to repent and believe then and there and no-one did so, our lack of success would be painfully obvious. We would be forced to admit to failure. So we avoid potential embarrassment by not asking for any definite response.

This approach can be defended by ingenious evasions, all truthful as far as they go. 'People may come to faith later. The Spirit works when and how he wishes, and the truth we have taught may well bear fruit in the future. We do not want to pressurise the unconverted into a hurried emotional response which falls short of saving faith. It is far better to explain the gospel and leave them to think it over at their leisure when they have time to reflect.' Do any of these sound familiar?

They are all true, of course, and can make our evangelism appear wonderfully biblical! But, in the context in which we tend to use them, these truths can be little more than sophistry, sops to our ministerial pride. As a boy, I used to smile at a notice in our local grocery shop: 'Please do not ask for credit, as a refusal often offends'. Yet how many gospel preachers have a similar warning posted on an inner wall of their consciousness: 'Please do not ask for a response, as a refusal may prove embarrassing'?

We need to throw off our self-protective dignity. We need to become far more vulnerable and acknowledge the pain of disappointment. It is certainly true that very often we will not know for some time, if ever on earth, whether or not our hearers have obeyed in faith. We do not need to know. Nor are we looking for any response which is merely outward and physical. The gospel of salvation calls for repentance and faith, inward spiritual graces, produced only by the power of God. The raised hand, the signed card, the coming forward, the effusive 'hallelujahs' so beloved of modern evangelicalism are at best froth, at worst delusion. What is sought is an inner transformation.

Yet this does not in any way negate our duty to call on our hearers to receive Christ—and to do so without delay. If there is no evidence that this has happened, let us weep for them, let us search our own hearts for causes of failure and, above all, let us fall on our knees in prayer for all who have so far rejected the gospel. But let us not deliberately avoid aiming at the target in case we miss it. We should not hesitate to issue the challenge because we are afraid that it may be rejected.

Terms such as repentance and faith will need to be explained. The condensed version of his preaching which we have in Acts does not show us in what ways Peter expanded on his call to repent and believe. Luke tells us that, before people were baptised on the day of Pentecost, 'with many other words he testified and exhorted them, saying, "Be saved from this perverse generation" ' (*Acts* 2:40). It would be impossible, of course, as well as unwise, to attempt in one evangelistic sermon a complete exposition of all that is involved in coming to Christ. Yet we should spell out the basics, the ABC of salvation. Our hearers should know what we mean and how they should obey. We need to make it as easy as possible for the unconverted to know precisely what it is that God is commanding them to do.

This will reinforce enormously the challenge of our preaching. People may reject the message we bring. But, if they do, they will stand condemned by their own consciences. They will never be able to say that they did not know how to obey. They rejected Christ because they did not want him. He urged them to come, but they were not willing.

11

Spirit-filled preaching

The most important element in Peter's preaching is also the most mysterious. A divine influence accompanied his words. God breathed from heaven upon his sermons and made them vehicles of grace. This phenomenon has been known in the history of preaching as unction—'anointing'. Peter the preacher was anointed in an unusual measure with the power of the Holy Spirit.

Christ had promised such an enabling to his apostles: 'You shall be baptized with the Holy Spirit not many days from now . . . You shall receive power when the Holy Spirit has come upon you: and you shall be witnesses to Me' (1:5,8). In due course, the promise was fulfilled when 'they were all filled with the Holy Spirit' (2:4) and it was under his influence that Peter and the others spoke: 'Then Peter, filled with the Holy Spirit, said to them . . .' 'They were all filled with the Holy Spirit, and they spoke the word of God with boldness' (4:8,31). This goes a long way towards explaining the effect-iveness of Peter's ministry. His preaching was Spirit-filled.

What does that mean? Like any other aspect of God's direct working, unction is hard to define. It needs to be experienced before it can be understood. Counterfeits abound. Many today claim to be speaking and acting under the direct influence of the Holy Spirit. But their unbiblical teaching and bizarre behaviour show little evidence of God's character. Others have almost turned the anointing of the Spirit into an idol. They attribute to it a prominence beyond that warranted from Scripture and see it as the panacea for most of the ills of the church and the world. Imbalance of this kind could make us wary of seeking such an experience for ourselves.

It is also true that certain features of the account in Acts were unique to the apostolic era. One result of the Holy Spirit's filling on the day of Pentecost was that the apostles 'began to speak with other tongues, as the Spirit gave them utterance' (2:4). Such miraculous happenings marked a new stage in the history of redemption. They are no more to be looked for today than are the 'sound from heaven, as of a rushing mighty wind' or the appearance of 'divided tongues, as of fire' (2:2,3).

Yet it is clear that Spirit-filled preaching has been a reality throughout the history of the church. We need only read accounts of great revivals and of men like Jonathan Edwards and George Whitefield to satisfy ourselves that unction did not end with the apostles. Nor is it granted only to the giants of the pulpit, for most true preachers have had experience of this marvellous enabling. Its coming is unpredictable, often unexpected. Suddenly the minister's heart is aflame and his words seem clothed with a new power. The congregation is strangely hushed or moved. There is a palpable sense of the presence of God. The Spirit exercises a melting, penetrating influence, so that all are aware that momentous issues are before them. In the words of an old Scottish preacher: 'There is sometimes somewhat in preaching that cannot be described either to matter or expression, and cannot be described what it is, or from whence it cometh, but with a sweet violence it pierceth into the heart and affections and comes immediately from the Lord.'[1] Such an experience is unforgettable, addictive, a day of heaven on earth. Once a preacher has known the richness of God's enabling, he can never again rest satisfied without it.

This is why men who have been greatly used in preaching the gospel lay such emphasis on seeking unction.[2] Martyn Lloyd-Jones describes it as 'the greatest essential in connection with preaching'.[3] 'This makes true preaching,' he says,

---

[1] Quoted in Douglas F. Kelly, *Preachers with Power* (Banner of Truth Trust, 1992), p. 168.

[2] See, for example, Spurgeon, *Lectures to My Students*, 'The Holy Spirit in connection with our ministry', pp. 185–204; *An All-Round Ministry* (Banner of Truth Trust, 1965), 'The preacher's power and the conditions of obtaining it' (pp. 315–63).

[3] *Preaching and Preachers*, p. 304.

'and it is the greatest need of all today—never more so. Nothing can substitute for this. Seek it until you have it; be content with nothing less.'[1]

That preacher is in a pitiable condition who can continue year after year without the breath of God upon his ministry. He is not alive enough to know his deadness. He knows too little of preaching to realise that he is not preaching. His lack of concern is his condemnation. God spare us from such awful futility!

We must seek unction. We must forsake every sin which might quench or grieve the Spirit. We need to feel, as never before, our utter dependence upon God. Without the power of the Holy Spirit, our preaching is ineffective. How often have we spoken lifelessly and coldly about the most glorious realities in the universe! Or perhaps we have entered the pulpit with warm hearts and high expectations, only to be chilled and depressed by an indifferent audience. What a stale, unprofitable thing it is to preach only in our own strength or to apathetic people! How exhausted and miserable it makes us! Robert Murray M'Cheyne used to write 'Master, help!' on his sermon manuscripts. Nothing is more important, surely, than that we should pray for such help in preaching the gospel.

The last chapter of John Angell James' stirring book *An Earnest Ministry the Want of the Times* is entitled 'The necessity of divine influence to make the ministry efficient'. It is a thrilling exhortation and several excerpts may give the flavour of the whole.

James challenges ministers to seek this anointing in the following words:

Is our conviction of dependence upon the Spirit so deep, practical, and constant, as to prevent us from attempting anything in our own strength, and make us feel strong only in the Lord and in the power of his might? Do we go to our pulpit in a praying frame, as well as in a preaching one; praying even while we preach, for our people as well as ourselves? Do we thus clothe ourselves with Omnipotence? . . . Do we recollect that from all that crowd of immortal souls before us . . . not one dark mind will be illumined, not one hard heart

[1] Ibid., p. 325.

[92]

softened, not one inquiring soul directed, not one wounded spirit healed, not one uneasy conscience appeased, unless God the Spirit do it? How entire, how confident, how believing should be our sense of dependence . . .![1]

We can pray confidently for such assistance from God because it is not something exotic or unusual, reserved for exceptional times and persons:

There is every ground to expect the influence we need. It is our privilege to live under the dispensation of the Spirit . . . This idea . . . should enlarge our expectations of rich communications of this invaluable and essential blessing . . . While God reserves to himself the right of bestowment . . . he warrants and invites the most comprehensive requests and the largest anticipations . . . Instead of being surprised that so much of this divine power accompanies the ministry in the most successful periods of our history, we should be surprised that we receive so little of it, and enquire after the obstructing cause.[2]

We have been thinking of various factors present in Peter's preaching of the gospel. But we are not of Peter's stature. Most of us lack his insight, his force of character, his natural gifts. Yet in the final analysis this need not matter, for the Almighty delights to work through the weakest human instruments. Our inadequacies are no barrier to the power of the gospel, provided that we have the Spirit. All we need to do is ask, for 'If you then, being evil, know how to give good gifts to your children, how much more will your heavenly Father give the Holy Spirit to those who ask Him!' (*Luke* 11:13).

The Spirit will endow us with all the qualities which we have admired in Peter's ministry. He will sharpen our wits and our sensitivities so that we will know how to speak to our hearers at the most urgent point of their need. He delights to honour the Son, for Jesus said that 'He will glorify Me, for He will take of what is Mine and declare it to you' (*John* 16:14). All Spirit-filled preaching, then, will have Christ at its centre. Empow-

---

[1] John Angell James, *An Earnest Ministry* (Banner of Truth Trust, 1993), pp. 290–1.
[2] Ibid., pp. 287–8

ered by him, we will be bold and direct, as the fear of man vanishes in an awareness of God's presence. When nothing else can move hard hearts, his life-giving influence will bring lost sinners to the Saviour in penitence and trust.

With his fullness, our preaching will be transformed:

We should derive from it an unspeakable advantage in addressing our hearers; a seriousness, tenderness, and majesty, beyond what the greatest unassisted talent could command, would pervade our discourses; a superhuman influence would rest upon us; a Divine glory would irradiate us; and we should speak in the power and demonstration of the Spirit.[1]

[1] Ibid., p. 291.

PETER THE PASTOR

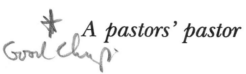

12

A pastors' pastor

Good Chap

Too many pastors are in trouble. Some are bewildered by conflicting expectations. Do their congregations want them to be teachers, administrators, psychiatrists, social workers or just everyone's friend? Are they meant to fulfil all these roles at once? Physical breakdown and nervous strain have taken their toll of others. Not a few have left the pastorate altogether, disillusioned with the calling upon which they had entered so expectantly. There is a crisis of confidence in ministerial ranks.

I could not help reflecting on this loss of morale recently as I looked at a young man sitting in my study. He was nervous but very much in earnest and had come to tell me that he believed that God was calling him into the ministry. I was not surprised, as I had known him for years and had watched his gifts developing. Yet my feelings were mixed, as I listened to him. I was thrilled, of course. What pastor would not be pleased at hearing such news from a member of his congregation? But at the same time I was apprehensive. While his idealism touched me, I worried about his vulnerability. Did he know what he could be letting himself in for? Would he be able to cope with the pressures? Might he be sitting in my study again in a few years, like other men I had known, unhappy and ready to give up?

Churches are complaining of a shortage of candidates for the pastorate. Yet the task of caring for God's people is one of the greatest privileges on earth. Why is it seen as a burden? What is going wrong?

One factor, at a superficial level, is the way in which the ministry is now perceived. The minister was once ranked with the doctor, the schoolmaster and the lawyer as a person of standing in the community. He was a professional, respected by society at large. But that time has long passed. People today have little awareness of God and regard the Bible as obsolete. This means that they have no concept of what the ministry is about. At best, they see the pastor as a rather ineffective do-gooder, pre-occupied with trivialities. It is not an appealing career prospect! How many men of normal ambition want to spend their lives in a calling where they will be patronised or ignored?

More serious is lack of appreciation within the church. Many Christians, who should know better, resent the authority of their pastors and undervalue their expertise. Some ministers create their own problems by clumsiness or impatience. Others, to their credit, are trying to reform their congregations. But they find that the process of correcting abuses or implementing discipline can make them unpopular and, in some cases, bring down upon them a tempest of fury. Behind everything else is the activity of Satan, who directs his fiercest attacks against Christian leaders.

Whatever the pressures, today's pastors need help. Where is it to be found? We might begin by studying some of the classics of pastoral theology. Ministerial conferences or short-term refresher courses can widen our insights and sharpen our skills. But what we need above all is someone to sit down with us and be our teacher. He should be an experienced pastor. He must know Christ and love people. It would help if, like ourselves, he had made his own share of mistakes. Yet we want him to be convinced of his calling and able to speak with authority. God has given us such a man—the apostle Peter.

His credentials are beyond question, because he was commissioned directly by Christ. When the Good Shepherd had risen from the grave and was about to return to heaven, he entrusted to Peter the care of his flock: 'Simon, son of Jonah, do you love me? Feed my lambs. Tend my sheep' (*John* 21:15,16). Never has a man received a clearer call to office. Nor has anyone taken a more impressive course in pastoral theology, for Peter's instructor was Jesus. It was the Lord who had taught him and prayed for him. After his great sin, it was the One whom he had denied who brought him to repentance, assured him of forgiveness and restored him to service. Peter learned how to be a pastor in the best possible way— from the Saviour's dealings with his soul. A transformed man, he devoted the rest of his life to bringing to others the grace which he himself had received. Here is someone to whom we can listen with confidence.

Part of the way in which he carried on his pastoral ministry was by sending letters to a group of churches in what is now Turkey. It was a long time ago, but 1 and 2 Peter are as relevant today as when they were first written. Those first century believers in 'Pontus, Galatia, Cappadocia, Asia and Bithynia' (*1 Pet.* 1:1) were living in a situation remarkably similar to our own.

They were a people under pressure. In the early sixties of the first century, when the letters were written, Christians were becoming increasingly unpopular. They were not yet subject to systematic persecution, though that would soon come. But they lived in a pluralistic, immoral society which resented their dogmatic faith and uncompromising ethical standards. They were experiencing repeated harassment and it is significant that there are references to such unpleasantness in every chapter of 1 Peter (1:6–7, 2:12, 3:13–17, 4:12–19, 5:9). These verses have an uncomfortably contemporary ring.

To make matters worse, the church itself was being infiltrated by heresy. 2 Peter, for example, has a great deal to say about false teachers who were scoffing at the second coming of Christ and teaching a 'new morality' which was nothing more than the idolising of sinful desires (e.g. 3:1–8, 2:4–22). Their approach was subtle and plausible, but the end result was confusion among the spiritually unwary.

This background helps us to understand why Peter describes his readers as 'the pilgrims of the Dispersion' (*1 Pet.* 1:1). The word translated 'pilgrims' is a technical term for resident aliens, foreigners living temporarily in a country not their own. 'The Dispersion' means 'the scattering' and referred originally to Jews who had been driven from Israel, dispersed among the nations. They were a vulnerable minority, waiting for the time when God would bring them back together in their own homeland. When Peter calls Christians 'the pilgrims of the Dispersion', he is implying that they are the new Israel. They too are living in an alien environment, scattered strangers in the world.

All of this sounds familiar, because we are not living at a time when the church is strong or Christian influence powerful. Like those to whom the apostle wrote, believers today are a minority under siege. The world resents us and the professing church seems muddled and divided. So this pastor can help us! He understands the pressures our people face.

His letters are a treasure-house. Taken together, they provide a superb case-study of how to counsel the people of God. He comes as a father, wise and tender. Practical commands flow naturally from profound doctrines. His theology is God-centred to the core and he holds realism and hope in perfect balance. Any minister would profit from studying these chapters in depth, both as food for his soul and guidance for his work.

Yet within the whole body of his teaching is one passage which is specially valuable, because it gives us the essence of Peter's pastoral instruction. He is now an old man, 'knowing that shortly I must put off my tent' (*2 Pet.* 1:14). As his ministry draws to a close, he wants to hand on to others the pastoral charge which Christ committed to him. He addresses 'the elders'—all, whether ordained ministers or not, who have been appointed to shepherd God's people. 1 Peter 5:1–4 is a perfect summary of what we need to remember and to these verses we now turn.

As always, context is important—and there is a word which many of our translations unaccountably leave out: 'the elders, therefore, who are among you.' This 'therefore' looks back to the previous paragraph. Peter's counsel to elders 'to shepherd the flock of God' does not come out of the blue but follows from what has gone before. It is a consequence of something just mentioned. To what is he referring?

He has been dealing, in 4:12–19, with the suffering which is caused by a hostile world. 'Beloved, do not think it strange concerning the fiery trial which is to try you . . .rejoice to the extent that you partake of Christ's sufferings . . .If you are reproached for the name of Christ, blessed are you . . . On their part he is blasphemed . . .if anyone suffers as a Christian, let him not be ashamed' (4:12,13,14,16). From this point he continues: 'The elders, therefore, I exhort'. What is the connection?

He is reminding us that leadership is never more crucial than when believers are under attack. It is then that Christian people will look to their elders most of all, just as sheep need their shepherd when the wolf comes near. His 'therefore' is a link with this crisis. It calls the elders to redouble their efforts and devote themselves with a new intensity to the welfare of the flock. It provides the basis for the exhortation which he is about to give.

But it is more than exhortation. There is also a sobering warning. The beginning of verse 17 reads: 'For the time has come for judgment to begin at the house of God . . it begins with us first.' Peter is here drawing on several Old Testament passages which speak of God coming to judge sin. When he does so come, however, he will not begin with the heathen, as we might expect. His judgment will commence with his own people, specifically with unfaithful leaders, and in the temple which they have polluted by their idolatry. In Ezekiel 9:6, for example, God tells the messengers of destruction to 'begin at My sanctuary. So they began with the elders. Malachi brings the same message: 'The Lord, whom you seek, will suddenly come to his temple. He will purify the sons of Levi, and purge them as gold and silver' (*Mal.* 3:1,3). Let the elders of the churches be alerted. God is using the fires of persecution to purify his people and his judgment will fall first upon any leaders who have been unfaithful to their trust. It is time for them to take their duties seriously. 'The elders, therefore, who are among you I exhort . . . shepherd the flock of God'.

Here then is Peter's advice to pastors in its most concentrated form. Let us listen, as he preaches to us. The apostle will deal with four areas of the pastor's life: his identity, his duty, his heart and his reward.

13

The pastor's identity

'I who am a fellow-elder and a witness of the sufferings of Christ, and also a partaker of the glory that will be revealed'.

Who is this teacher of pastors? What are his qualifications? We are naturally more disposed to pay attention to people we respect than to those in whom we have little confidence. So Peter begins by describing himself. As we listen, we will find that he is eminently equipped to be our instructor. Here is someone who deserves to be heard and obeyed. But in describing himself he also describes us, for he places himself among us. As we understand who Peter is, we will learn who we are meant to be. Three luminous phrases express his identity—and ours.

i. *'I who am a fellow-elder'*
This is one of 'the Twelve' speaking. He was a member of that uniquely privileged group of men whom Christ chose to be his disciples. They were closer to Jesus of Nazareth than the members of his own family. For three years they lived and travelled with him, saw his miracles and heard his teaching. He took them into his confidence and revealed to them those secrets of the kingdom which Old Testament prophets and kings had longed to know. Not only so, but Peter, with James and John, formed a select group within the Twelve. These were Jesus' special friends. He took them with him to the Mount of Transfiguration and into the Garden of Gethsemane. On many occasions they were admitted to an intimacy denied to the others. What an honour was theirs!

Then, when the Lord was about to return to heaven, he raised the disciples to even higher honour. As 'apostles', they

[102]

were his appointed representatives, clothed with his authority and sent out in his name. Their task was to go into all the world with the gospel. The church itself was founded upon them and Peter was the leader of them all. It was he who presided in their early gatherings. It was he who took the keys and opened the kingdom of heaven to sinners on the day of Pentecost and in the home of the Gentile Cornelius. He is in the very first rank of the leaders of the Christian church.

Yet, when he writes to ordinary elders in local congregations, he lays no emphasis on the dignity of his position, but describes himself simply as 'a fellow-elder'. He is not coming to them as a superior, but as an equal. He is stressing what identifies him with his readers, not what distinguishes him from them. What they are to focus on is the office which he and they hold in common.

Such humility is as admirable as it is rare. Christ's comment on religious leaders who elbow their way to 'the best seats in the synagogue' (*Luke* 11:43) still stings as it makes us smile. The generation of pompous clerics has not yet passed away. How silly are the manoeuvres by which some men try to make sure that they are noticed! How ridiculous to see a minister more concerned with his own dignity than with the glory of the most high God whom he claims to serve! A lovely incident in the life of James S. Stewart illustrates a better spirit. The noted preacher, academic and writer had been invited to a reception in Edinburgh where he was to receive a citation for his contribution to Christian literature. When he drove into the car-park, a policeman who did not recognise him asked him to leave, as the spaces were reserved for VIPs. The guest of honour quietly drove off and parked elsewhere.

Peter has no time for the nonsense of ecclesiastical one-up-manship, but follows his own advice not to 'lord it' over others (5:3). Here is the modesty of greatness, more comfortable among believers than above them.

In other words, he is about to preach to himself. This teaching is for 'the elders' and Peter is an elder, not a detached observer. He will listen to his own sermon. He will sit in the congregation to which he is speaking. We cannot help warming to a man who is so clearly subject to the very Word which he preaches to others.

[103]

But there is more than humility in this self-description. Peter, we have said, brings himself down to the level of his hearers. But he might protest that he is doing exactly the opposite. If an apostle can sit among elders, then surely elders may sit among apostles. Instead of lowering himself he may be raising them. If Peter is content to describe himself in this way, then the eldership must be a significant and responsible calling. A position held by one of the most privileged associates of our Lord cannot be a trivial one, reserved for the second-rate. These anonymous elders are colleagues of the great apostle!

Nothing would raise the morale of ministers more quickly than a renewed awareness of the dignity of their office. They are undervalued. We have seen that society has a low estimate of the pastor and churches themselves, without meaning to, can contribute to this. Hierarchical denominations have a career structure through which a man may hope to progress. Beginning with the care of a single congregation, he can end up as a bishop overseeing a diocese. Might this create the impression that service in a local fellowship is merely the lowest rung on the ladder of promotion?

Nonconformist churches with no such hierarchy can still have their own pecking order. When a large, influential congregation is seen as a more prestigious charge than a remote and struggling one, the pastorate is undervalued. When a man takes pride in many invitations to preach away from home, he is forgetting the glory of his calling. A church which absorbs its more talented leaders into a central bureaucracy has mistaken its priorities.

An increasing trend is for gifted ministers to be siphoned into theological colleges. Now that may not be wrong in itself, for the training of pastors is a very worthwhile task. We do well to honour and pray for all who are involved in it. But the rationale sometimes offered for the recruitment of such men is troubling. The suggestion is that their unusual intellectual or preaching abilities deserve a wider platform than the pastorate can offer. No-one may be crass enough to say that they are wasted where they are. But the impression is given that a move is equivalent to promotion.

Such a mentality is misguided. Candidates for the ministry

certainly deserve the most competent instruction available. But the front-line troops of the kingdom of God are the leaders in the churches. Here is where the body of Christ is built up and where the gospel reaches the world. Here is where the battle is lost or won. A pastor has a sphere of influence in the lives of his people and in his community which is almost unlimited. He will not complain at the day of judgment that his opportunities were too narrow. Preaching the Word and caring for the flock demand all the gifts, and more, which anyone can bring to them. We must insist that the place for our best ministers is in the churches.

In describing himself as an elder Peter focuses our attention on the essential office, not the attendant circumstances. A man may be called to a travelling or specialist ministry. He may pastor theological students. Most should take their place in a local congregation. But what is important is to esteem equally all who hold the office. There can be no greater honour on earth than to serve as an elder in the church of Christ.

ii. 'A witness of the sufferings of Christ'

Peter had seen with his own eyes the sufferings of Jesus. He saw murderous hatred etched on the faces of the Pharisees. He heard their sneers and the ugly rumours with which they tried to discredit his Master. As Christ travelled through Palestine with the Twelve, he was often physically exhausted and emotionally drained. The unbelief of those to whom he preached grieved him. Every time he looked at human lives wrecked by sin, his heart was moved with compassion. The disciples must have perceived something of the price he was paying, because Jesus was open with them. Unlike some leaders, he felt no compulsion to pose as a superman, impervious to pain. Those close to him would see him, in measure at least, as 'a man of sorrows and acquainted with grief' (*Isa.* 53:3).

In Gethsemane, 'He took Peter, James and John with him, and he began to be troubled and deeply distressed. Then he said to them, My soul is exceedingly sorrowful, even to death' (*Mark* 14:33,34). How alarming these words must have been! His friends must have felt like children who see, for the first time, their father weeping. It was an earthquake in their emotional world. Here was the strong one, on whom they all depended, now acknowledging a mortal sorrow. Were they awake long enough to hear the repeated prayer of agony: 'Father, if it is your will, remove this cup from me; nevertheless not my will but yours be done' (*Luke* 22:42)? Did they see 'his sweat like great drops of blood falling down to the ground' (*Luke* 22:44)? They knew at any rate that this was an hour of most intense suffering.

After Gethsemane came the palace of the high priest, where Christ was falsely accused, mocked and spat upon. Roman soldiers drove thorns into his scalp and tore open his back with the dreaded punishment flail. Peter was there and saw much of what happened. At Calvary he was not among the group standing near the cross, for he had denied his Lord and had fled weeping into the darkness. But Luke tells us that, as Jesus hung there, 'all his acquaintances, and the women who followed him from Galilee, stood at a distance, watching these things' (*Luke* 23:49). We can picture Peter, still far off but watching with a breaking heart. With tear-filled eyes he saw his dying Master nailed to the tree, and in the darkness, he heard the cry of desolating agony.

'A witness of the sufferings of Christ'. Yes! Terribly, unforgettably. The memory of those hours was branded on his consciousness for ever.

So when he wrote: 'You were redeemed . . . with the precious blood of Christ' (*1 Pet.* 1:18,19), it was from a vivid awareness of the price paid for our salvation. Christ's blood was no abstraction or cliché to Peter, for in his mind's eye he could see it still. It spurred him constantly to faithfulness. If Jesus gave his life for the church, how could Peter shrink from any suffering which his own ministry might bring?

For all Christian service carries an inevitable price-tag. Although some of the sufferings of the Son of God at Calvary were unique and unrepeatable, there is a sense in which others continue in the lives of his people. 'Rejoice', wrote Peter to harassed believers, 'to the extent that you partake of Christ's sufferings' (*1 Pet.* 4:13). He had experienced these sufferings for himself. The Book of Acts records how the apostle had been beaten, threatened and thrown into prison.

There were more to come, for Jesus had prophesied his violent death, in itself an act of discipleship: 'When you are old, you will stretch out your hands, and another will dress you and carry you where you do not wish. This he spoke, signifying by what death he would glorify God. And when he had spoken this, he said to him, Follow me' (*John* 21:18,19).

We may say in fact that Peter was 'a witness of the sufferings of Christ' in a double sense. On one hand, he had seen them for himself. On the other, he had experienced them in his own body. A witness can mean either someone who sees or someone who helps others to see. When the writer to the Hebrews reminds us that 'we are surrounded by so great a cloud of witnesses' (*Heb.* 12:1), he is using the word in its second sense. The idea is not that we are surrounded by a multitude of heavenly beings who are constantly watching us. It is rather that the lives of the heroes of chapter eleven are monuments, erected to remind us of what living by faith really involves. They are 'witnesses' in that they enable us to see what might otherwise be invisible.

Peter is an elder who has seen for himself the sufferings of Christ. In his life and person he also makes plain those sufferings to others. Such a man is a credible teacher. He deserves to be heard as he speaks about his work and ours.

He is more than a teacher, of course, for he is also setting us an example. All elders are to be 'witnesses of the sufferings of Christ'. It is true that we cannot go back in time and see them as the apostles did. But we can follow our fellow-elder by meditating constantly on Calvary. We can go to the Gospels, the epistles, the prophets and psalms and gaze upon the crucified One. In Scripture, we can survey the wondrous cross, prayerfully contemplating the Lamb of God until his sufferings become imprinted indelibly upon our very beings. As Robert Leighton wrote in his classic seventeenth-century commentary on 1 Peter: 'A spiritual view of Christ crucified is the thing that will bind upon us most strongly all the duties of our particular calling. It is the very life of the Gospel and of our souls.'[1]

---

[1] Robert Leighton, *Commentary on 1 Peter* (Grand Rapids: Kregel Publications, 1972), pp. 465–6.

As well as looking for ourselves, we can help others to see. Called day by day to share in Christ's sufferings, we will serve as witnesses in the secondary sense also. In April 1685, two Scottish Covenanters were sentenced to death by drowning because of their loyalty to Christ. Margaret MacLachlan was seventy years of age, Margaret Wilson was a girl of eighteen. The older woman was tied to a stake further out in the tidewater so that young Margaret might be terrified by her death struggle. But the persecutors had underestimated the faith of their prey. When Margaret Wilson, gazing at her friend, was asked, 'What do you think of her now?', her reply was magnificent: 'Think! I see Christ wrestling there. Think ye that we are sufferers? No; it is Christ in us.'

How encouraging for us to realise that in our pain we can reveal the Saviour! Is not that testimony being repeated all over the world today as people look at struggling, suffering leaders and say, with a sense of wonder, 'I see Christ wrestling there'? 'A witness of the sufferings of Christ'.

iii. 'A partaker of the glory that will be revealed'

In the early stages of his Christian life, Peter had found the concept of a suffering Messiah hard to accept. This was partly the fault of his upbringing. The Jewish people had been oppressed by foreigners for centuries. Roman domination of their country had fed a burning sense of injustice together with a passion for liberty. In these circumstances it was natural that they would politicise the prophecies of the Old Testament. The long-expected Messiah was seen as a victorious general. God's promised deliverer would bring in a new age of blessing by freeing them from their enemies. As the anointed of the Lord, his career could be marked only by unbroken success. They seem to have overlooked passages like Psalm 22 or Isaiah 53 which spoke of God's servant as a sufferer. Like his contemporaries, Peter inherited this triumphalist understanding of the hope of Israel.

This is why, as we have seen earlier, he was horrified to hear that the Messiah would have to suffer and die. 'Far be it from you, Lord,' he protested: 'this shall not happen to you!' (*Matt.*

16:22). A rejected Christ? It was a contradiction in terms. How could the Blessed One be killed by his own people? What would happen to God's salvation?

But Peter's perceptions were to change. Six days later Jesus took him, with James and John, to the mount of transfiguration where, he says: 'we were eyewitnesses of His majesty. For He received from God the Father honour and glory' (*2 Pet.* 1:16,17). Peter and his friends saw the Son of God in his heavenly glory. They were 'partakers, sharers' in it, to use his own word here. This glory, moreover, was linked, in a way he did not yet understand, with Christ's sufferings, for the radiant Saviour had been discussing with Moses and Elijah 'His decease which He was about to accomplish at Jerusalem' (*Luke* 9:31).

Slowly, reluctantly, Peter came to realise that the suffering was neither a mistake nor a tragedy. It was, rather, Christ's path to glory. The dreaded cross not only led past the grave to a crown of life but was the indispensable preliminary to that crown. Jesus would be glorified because of his suffering, not in spite of it.

And what was true of Christ must be true also for all who are in Christ. As we will see later, the hope of future glory is a key emphasis in Peter's pastoral teaching. He has already encouraged his readers along these lines in 4:13: 'Rejoice to the extent that you partake of Christ's sufferings, that when his glory is revealed, you may also be glad with exceeding joy'. The logic of his argument is clear. They can rejoice in the midst of suffering because their suffering is a guarantee of glory, a sign that they are sharers in Christ's destiny. Paul enunciates the same principle when he tells us that we are 'heirs of God and joint heirs with Christ, if indeed we suffer with him, that we may also be glorified together' (*Rom.* 8:17).

Now he applies the same truth to himself and his fellow-elders, because the 'witness of the sufferings of Christ' is also 'a partaker of the glory that will be revealed'. The elder will suffer. He is often called to travel a path of pain. But what makes it all worthwhile is that he is walking in the footsteps of the Lord who is now in glory. This is the authentic road to heaven. Christ's glory is largely unseen

[109]

as yet, but it will soon be 'revealed' and, when it is, he will share it with his servants.

Here is Peter's identity—and that of every true elder. What a privilege to have him as our pastor! What a privilege for any congregation to be shepherded by such a man!

14

The pastor's duty

'Shepherd the flock of God which is among you, serving as overseers'.
'Pastor' is the Latin word for 'shepherd' and Peter drives straight to the heart of an elder's duty with his opening words in verse 2: 'Shepherd the flock'. He is echoing his own commission from Christ—'Shepherd my sheep' (*John* 21:16, NASB)—and providing a perfect summary of what is involved. Pastors are to do for their people all that a shepherd does for his flock of sheep.

This biblical imagery is rich and suggestive and a few references provide only the barest outline. God is the shepherd of his people (*Psa.* 80:1). They are like sheep in their vulnerability and tendency to stray (*Isa.* 53:6). The shepherd will feed and water his sheep (*Psa.* 23:2). He will lead and protect them (*Psa.* 23:3,4) and search for them when they are lost (*Luke* 15:4–6). In the Old Testament, as well as in the New, human leaders were appointed as shepherds (*2 Sam.* 5:2), but the ultimate shepherd, the good shepherd, is the Lord Jesus Christ who gave his life for his sheep (*John* 10:11). From these and many other passages, elders can identify their areas of pastoral responsibility. A thorough study along such lines would certainly help us in assessing how adequately we are discharging our duties.

Peter, however, chooses to emphasise several more specific points in these verses and we note the following four:

i. The pastor's duty is of a specialised nature—'shepherd the flock'. There is a word-play in the original Greek—*poimanate to poimnion*—which is difficult to capture in English—'shepherd the sheep' or 'herd the herd', perhaps. The point is that both verb and noun come from the same root. The work to be done and those on whose behalf it is done are linked in the closest possible way.

We should not make too much of this linguistic feature. Yet it seems clear that the work of the pastor is inseparably connected with those whom he is called to serve. Everything he does must be crafted with them in mind. 'Who are my people? What stage have they reached? What do they really need? Where are they going?' Such questions must be asked in all aspects of pastoral duty. There can be nothing abstract or theoretical in the pastor's approach to his task. If he were a scientist, his work would be described as 'applied' rather than 'pure'. All has a practical purpose—the well-being of the flock.

The true pastor will spend many hours each week in his study. The tools of his trade are books on theology, biblical background and interpretation, church history and so on. These he will delight to use. Above all, he will devote himself to meditating on Scripture. But his reading will never be an end in itself. He will not study to become an expert in this or that branch of religious knowledge. His aim is to provide nourishing spiritual food for those who listen to him. It is always pastoral study.

His preaching will be pastoral preaching. As he prepares sermons, his people will be constantly before him. He is not interested in producing magnificent pieces of biblical interpretation for their own sake. His goal is more practical—to point sinners to the Saviour, guide the perplexed and strengthen the burdened.

A sign of a good pastoral preacher is that he finds it difficult to preach elsewhere a sermon originally composed for his own congregation. This is because his sermons are tailor-made. He prepares with individual customers in mind and always cuts the cloth of exposition and application to suit them exactly. When speaking in another situation, the material will need to be reworked. A few of his sermons will travel well, but they will be in the minority. 'One size fits all' has never been a slogan to inspire much confidence in those who want a new suit of clothes. Nor do ready-made sermons usually fit as snugly as those crafted by a man who knows his people.

This means that preaching and pastoring belong together.

We must, of course, protect the minister's hours of study. He should be allowed to give himself without distraction to preparing for the pulpit. He is not an errand-boy, at the beck and call of anyone who may want to claim his time. But some men have twisted their commitment to preaching into a rationale for pastoral neglect. They take a high-and-mighty tone about the primacy of the pulpit. As dedicated preachers they have no time, they say, to visit people and deal with their problems individually. They seem happy to accept the first part of the famous description of a minister: 'invisible on six days of the week and incomprehensible on the other'.

But this is either a misunderstanding or an excuse for social immaturity or laziness. We cannot preach adequately, on a continuing basis, to people whom we do not know. As the pastor visits in the congregation, he is made aware of needs and problems. Feedback from his people shows him to what extent his preaching is being understood. This will make him a better communicator. Then, when he stands in the pulpit, he will pastor the flock by providing food which is appropriate. Each aspect of the work reinforces the other.

One of the most challenging books ever written on the pastorate is *The Reformed Pastor* by Richard Baxter, vicar of Kidderminster from 1647 to 1661. It is, among other things, a plea to ministers to visit and catechise in the homes of their people. Baxter, in true Puritan style, provides twenty-two 'Motives to this Duty'. Among them, he cites the following benefits which will accrue to our preaching.

It will make our public preaching better understood and regarded . . . As you would not, therefore, lose your public labour, see that you be faithful in this private work. By means of it, you will come to be familiar with your people, and may thereby win their affections . . . When a minister knows not his people, or is as strange to them as if he did not know them, it must be a great hindrance to his doing any good among them. By means of it, we shall come to be better acquainted with each person's spiritual state, and so the better know how to watch over them. We shall know better how to preach to them, and carry ourselves to them, when we know their temper, and their chief objections, and so what they have most need to hear.[1]

[1] Richard Baxter, *The Reformed Pastor* (Banner of Truth Trust, 1974), pp. 177–8.

A good preacher or a good pastor? Both. We must not separate what God has joined. One way of making sure that we are not incomprehensible on the Lord's Day is to be reasonably visible on the other six.

This mindset is to dominate not just preaching but every part of the pastor's duty. He is always caring for the sheep. Everything is done for their sake and with their welfare in view. As one called to 'shepherd the flock', he finds his raison d'être in the people entrusted to his care. He is their pastor or he is nothing.

The implication for the preparation of pastors is obvious. Shepherds are trained by those who know what it is to care for sheep. In the same way, candidates for the ministry should be trained by instructors with adequate pastoral experience. There is a regrettable tendency today to overlook this and to entrust theological education to men who know little of congregational ministry. Their academic ability may be undoubted. Their teaching is often orthodox, brilliant, conversant with recent developments in biblical scholarship. None of this is to be despised. But something is missing. What they say cannot be 'earthed' in the soil of ministry, for they have never served in the pastoral ranks.

There is certainly a place for the professional scholar in ministerial education. He can offer elective courses, supplement basic instruction or serve as a 'post-graduate' resource for the more intellectually gifted. But it is a mistake to hand over a significant part of the training of pastors to men who have never done the work for which they are preparing others.

In his superb history of Princeton Seminary, David B. Calhoun comments perceptively on a debate over the seminary curriculum in the early years of this century. Princeton had always been renowned for its emphasis on the classical theological disciplines. At this time, however, a demand arose for more 'practical' courses. While this was due in the main to a growing anti-intellectualism, Calhoun suggests another contributory reason. Archibald Alexander and Samuel Miller, the first professors, had each spent almost twenty years in the pastorate before coming to the seminary. Some of their successors had little such experience and their teaching was correspondingly less adapted to pastoral realities. 'Princeton had maintained faithfully the founders' priorities in promoting "solid learning" and "piety of heart," but it had lost something of Alexander's and Miller's ability to teach and model for the students the skills of ministry.'[1]

The pastor should remember that he is called to be a specialist. His speciality is the care of his people and he must refuse to be side-tracked in any other direction, no matter how appealing.

ii. The pastor's duty is one of immense responsibility— 'the flock of God'.

This phrase reminds us of the identity of those whom we serve. What a description! They are God's own sheep, his people, chosen and loved from all eternity. In a culture based on sheep-rearing, a man's flock was his most precious possession. He would cherish it diligently and guard it with his life. The Old Testament writers exulted in the awareness that this was how God regarded Israel.

He made His own people go forth like sheep, And guided them in the wilderness like a flock . . . He will feed His flock like a shepherd; He will gather the lambs with His arm, And carry them in His bosom, And gently lead those who are with young . . . For thus says the Lord GOD: "Indeed I Myself will search for My sheep and seek them out. As a shepherd seeks out his flock on the day he is among his scattered sheep, so will I seek out My sheep and deliver them from all the places where they were scattered on a cloudy and dark day. And I will bring them out from the peoples and gather them from the countries, and will bring them to their own land; I will feed them on the mountains of Israel, in the valleys and in all the inhabited places of the country. I will feed them in good pasture, and their fold shall be on the high mountains of Israel. There they shall lie down in a good fold and feed in rich pasture on the mountains of Israel. I will feed My flock, and I will make them lie down," says the Lord GOD. "I will seek what was lost and bring back what was driven away, bind up the broken and strengthen what was sick" (*Psa.* 78:52; *Isa.* 40:11; *Ezek.* 34:11–16).

---

[1] David B. Calhoun, *Princeton Seminary: The Majestic Testimony* (Banner of Truth Trust, 1996), p. 269.

How intensely God loves his flock! How much care he devotes to their well-being! And it is this flock which is entrusted to pastors. We must never despise the Lord's people, never handle them impatiently or with distaste. They do not exist to feed our egos. They are not mere fodder for our grandiose schemes. They are 'the flock . . . the church of God which He purchased with His own blood' (*Acts* 20:28). As C. S. Lewis remarked, 'Christ told Peter to feed his sheep, not to teach new tricks to his performing rats.' We must never forget who they are and how great our responsibility. When God speaks through Ezekiel to the unfaithful 'shepherds' of Israel, his terrifyingly stern words seem to centre round the repeated phrase, piercing the conscience like a sword-thrust, 'My flock':

My sheep wandered through all the mountains, and on every high hill; yes, My flock was scattered over the whole face of the earth, and no-one was seeking or searching for them . . . As I live, says the Lord GOD, surely because My flock became a prey, and My flock became food for every beast of the field, because there was no shepherd, nor did My shepherds search for My flock, but the shepherds fed themselves and did not feed My flock . . . Behold, I am against the shepherds, and I will require My flock at their hand (*Ezek.* 34:6–10).

It is not always easy to keep this in mind, for a congregation may not look or act like the flock of God. Their peculiarities may be all too painfully clear. Their weaknesses and wanderings may exhaust those who try to help them. A pastor may feel that he is wasting his energies on a commonplace and insignificant group of people. He needs to keep praying all the more, then, that he may constantly see them through Christ's eyes. This perception alone will enable him to care for the church as he should.

When Jesus was commissioning Peter to the pastorate, it is significant that he did not ask him, 'Do you love my sheep?' It was important, of course, that Peter should love the sheep, but such affection was not to provide the impetus for his ministry. The question was, rather, 'Simon, son of Jonah, do you love Me?' (*John* 21:16). Here is the secret. If we love the Saviour, we will be able to shepherd his sheep. No matter how

[116]

unimpressive they may sometimes appear, they are his and we love them for his sake.

iii. The pastor's duty requires intimate contact—'which is among you'.

Although R. C. H. Lenski translates this phrase as 'in your care' and the NIV's 'under your care' agrees, the older version is preferable. Not only is it more literal, but the same expression is found in verse one where 'in your care' would make no sense—'the elders who are among you'. The people know their elders. Before electing them to office, the members of the congregation examined their character, home life and spiritual gifts. Those chosen were not remote figures but friends, from 'among' them. In the same way, the shepherds are in close contact with the flock. They see the sheep constantly, moving about among them, intimately involved in their lives, not withdrawn in any way. They are not coldly objective professionals, caring for their charges by remote control. Their work is 'hands-on', close range. It cannot be managed by tele-communication.

This is where 'serving as overseers' comes in. The 'overseer' (*episkopos*) was a watcher. In classical Greek the term referred to someone appointed to look after a business or superintend a piece of construction work. It was used for those officials whom Athens sent to supervise the affairs of smaller cities under its control. When the house of the Lord was being repaired in the reign of Josiah, those in charge of the teams of workmen were called overseers (*2 Chron.* 34:12). An essential part of their work was a close, penetrating scrutiny of what was actually happening.

The same idea carries over into the New Testament use of the word. The writer of Hebrews, for example, urges his readers to 'Pursue peace . . . and holiness . . . looking diligently lest anyone fall short of the grace of God' (12:14,15). 'Looking diligently', the same word as 'serving as overseers' here, 'expresses', says B. F. Westcott, 'the careful regard of those who occupy a position of responsibility'. The overseer is someone responsible for examining, regarding carefully, looking diligently.

A pastor, therefore, is obliged by his office to keep himself informed about the lives of his people. We know that every believer is a priest, able to approach God directly, without any human intermediary. We agree that each person is responsible for his or her own spiritual development. It is true that some elders have developed into spiritual bullies, far too inquisitive about matters which are none of their concern. Intrusiveness into the private affairs of an individual is unhealthy and Christians should resist any such invasion. It is a denial of the truth that 'each of us shall give account of himself to God' (*Rom.* 14:12).

Yet the culture in which we live has taken this respect for the dignity of the individual to an absurd extreme. The rights and freedom of each human being are seen as inviolable, unless of course they are unborn, elderly or otherwise in the way. Our age hates authority more than most. People resent any supervision or advice from outside themselves. Every man is his own law, subject only to his own judgment. The individual, created in glory by God, has become a monster, grotesque and deadly.

This rebellious arrogance has infected the church. It is being suggested more and more, for example, that a pastor has no right to interfere in any way with the private lives of his people. What they decide to do does not concern him. He does not need to know very much about them. His task is to preach the Word, apply it in general terms and make himself available to help when asked. Any more direct involvement is interpreted as impertinent meddling.

But how does a shepherd 'oversee' his sheep? He comes close to them and examines them. He looks for cuts, lameness or parasites. He runs his hands through a sheep's fleece, holds up its head and gazes deeply into its eyes, watching for signs of malnutrition or disease. Without a careful, frequent study of each animal he simply cannot do his work. The sheep itself may not always welcome this close inspection and may try to wriggle free. But the shepherd is not being aggressive or intrusive. He is motivated, rather, by love and concern. He is there to help and overseeing is an essential part of that helping process.

In the same way, it is appropriate for a pastor to be interested in his people. A great part of their lives will be none of his business and he will have no desire to pry. But he will look for signs of illness or malnutrition. He will note a tendency to wander. He will be concerned about those who are quarrelsome or chronically isolated. When necessary he will take decisive action to deal with problems. All this will require close dealing. It may at times seem unwelcome, even threatening. But in the long run his people will be thankful for the courage and compassion of a man who loves them too much to leave them in their sin and need.

The duties of shepherding and overseeing provide a perfect balance. A minister who does not feed his people in love has no moral right to supervise their lives. Anyone, on the other hand, who does not oversee, who is not personally involved with and informed about his sheep, is in no position to feed them properly. He does not deserve the name of pastor.

iv. The pastor's duty is given to him by God's sovereign disposing— 'those entrusted to you' (5:3).
This phrase could be translated literally 'the lots', a meaning captured in the NASB 'those allotted to your charge'. It is the word used in the Greek version of the Old Testament for the portions of Israel which were assigned by lot to tribes and families. The term 'inheritance' comes from the same word-group, for the two ideas were closely linked. As God told Moses: 'The land shall be divided by lot; they shall inherit according to the names of the tribes of their fathers. According to the lot their inheritance shall be divided between the larger and the smaller' (*Num.* 26:55,56).

These 'lots', or pieces of ground, varied greatly. Some were in fertile land, some in barren or rocky soil. Some were large, some much smaller. Some were near the trade routes or close to cities, others in very remote situations. To return to the shepherd metaphor, some places may have had rich pasture and plentiful water-supply, others very little. Some flocks may have been large and healthy, others composed of a few ill-bred weaklings.

Doubtless there were times when Israelites looked enviously at the inheritance of another tribe or family and wished that it were theirs. But in their better moments they would remember that the lots had been distributed by the sovereign wisdom of the Lord. Each one, even the poorest, was an immense blessing, a share in the promised land of Canaan. They should receive it with gratitude and care for it diligently. To complain or grumble would be wickedness indeed.

This provides a helpful model for pastors as they think of their spheres of duty. Their 'lot' may be either a congregation as a whole or an area of work within a congregation. Far-off fields look green and it is all too easy to become discontented when we look at the opportunities enjoyed by others. A man may see a brother minister with a large church, gifted office-bearers, a united, prayerful people and many open doors for outreach. It may all contrast painfully with his own more limited or discouraging circumstances. One elder may thrill the crowds with his eloquent expositions, while another has to toil behind the scenes in counselling or administration. The temptations to envy, self-pity and discontent are subtle and strong.

But we need to remember that we are where the Lord has placed us and where he wants us to be. He has appointed our sphere of labour and our task is to be faithful. We should not be discouraged at difficult circumstances. Perhaps he chooses to send his best men to the dangerous, barren outposts of the kingdom. Above all, we are in the promised land, inheritors of the blessing. How much better to spend our lives tending a rocky outcrop in Israel than to grow fat in the rich flatlands of doomed Egypt! Every pastor should be able to look at those entrusted to him and say with David: 'You, O LORD, are the portion of my inheritance and my cup; You maintain my lot. The lines have fallen to me in pleasant places; Yes, I have a good inheritance' (*Psa.* 16:5,6).

Columba was an Irish churchman who took the gospel to western Scotland in the sixth century. In one of his prayers he looks forward to heaven. He is perhaps reflecting on Psalm 84:10: 'I would rather be a doorkeeper in the house of my God than dwell in the tents of wickedness'. But his thoughts are equally applicable to the pastor as he thinks of earthly service in the church of Christ:

[120]

The pastor's duty

Almighty Father, Son and Holy Ghost,
Eternal, ever-blessed gracious God,
To me, the least of saints, to me allow
That I may keep a door in Paradise;
That I may keep even the smallest door,
The furthest door, the darkest coldest door,
The door that is least used, the stiffest door,
If so it be but in thine house, O God!
If so it be that I can see thy glory
Even afar and hear thy voice, O God!
And know that I am with thee—thee, O God.

Here is the pastor's duty: to share in the leadership which Christ provides for his precious flock; to serve them on his behalf. It is a glorious and awesome responsibility.

15

The pastor's heart

'Not by constraint but willingly, according to God, not for dishonest gain but eagerly; nor as being lords over those entrusted to you, but being examples to the flock.'

When the prophet Samuel was looking for a new king for Israel among the sons of Jesse he was greatly impressed by the unusual height and majestic presence of Eliab, the first-born. God, however, had a more penetrating perspective and reminded him that 'man looks at the outward appearance, but the LORD looks at the heart' (*1 Sam.* 16:7). That remains as true for pastors as it was for kings. God's chief concern is with the pastor's heart—his motivation, his inner attitude and also the spirit in which he carries out his work. He is not only interested in what we do, but perhaps even more in how and why we do it.

We need this reminder in a society where preoccupation with technique and visible efficiency is affecting the church to an increasing extent. Modern pastors are well schooled in the mechanics of their profession. Many of them have taken courses in administration and time-management. They draw up organisational charts and understand the ways in which group dynamics can be harnessed to promote trouble-free meetings. In a word, they are professionals. This need not, of course, be a bad thing. God is not glorified by sloppiness and his servants should be seen to be competent in all that they do. But there is a real danger that, in all this focus upon visible performance and polish, something vital may be missed.

Peter brings us back to what is primary. 'What sort of men are you?' he asks. 'What is in your hearts? What is the ethos, the prevailing temper of mind in which you live and serve? As you move among your people, how do you really feel about your calling?' 'The LORD looks at the heart' and what he finds there will determine the extent to which our ministry is acceptable and effective.

Peter mentions three dangers, professional hazards, to which pastors are peculiarly subject and urges us to avoid them.

i. 'Not by constraint but willingly, according to God.'

There is a constraint from God which is proper and without which no-one should enter the pastoral office. Paul referred to it when he wrote, 'Necessity is laid upon me; yes, woe is me if I do not preach the gospel' (*1 Cor.* 9:16). He felt an inner compulsion, a powerful sense of divine calling. He was a gospel preacher because of God's appointing and this is the experience of every true pastor. Only such an overwhelming necessity enables a man to overcome his sense of unworthiness and inadequacy. Only such a heavenly summons will sustain him in times of discouragement. He is where he is because God has placed him there. This is his warrant and authority for ministry.

Nor is this constraint at all unwelcome. On the contrary, the pastor delights in his calling. It is for him a never-failing source of amazement and gladness. He would never have presumed to aspire to the ministry were he not convinced that it was God's purpose for him. Yet this is at the same time the very work for which he has longed with all his being. Powerfully constrained, yet totally willing, he freely chooses to do what he knows to be the inescapable will of God. Such a compulsion from his Saviour both empowers and satisfies him. He finds the yoke of Christ easy and his burden light. Peter is not warning about that kind of constraint.

He is thinking, rather, of a reluctant, grudging service. What he has in mind is an elder who carries out his duties hesitantly, resentfully, against his will. His heart is not in his work. He does it only because he feels he must.

We may think that this is not a major problem today. It used to be the custom for young men to be destined for the church without any apparent awareness of the need for a divine call. In the stately homes of England the eldest boy would inherit the property. Younger sons would be placed in the army, the law or the clergy, whether they had any inclination in those directions or not. The results, in church life at least, were predictably disastrous. Many a Scots mother informed her infant son that he had been dedicated from birth to the ministry and that it was her heart's desire to live to see him in his own pulpit. Such misdirected enthusiasm, while sometimes overruled by God for good, undoubtedly did result in ministerial misfits. Men found themselves in the pastorate with neither aptitude nor God-honouring motivation. There was even the cynical but, sadly, not unfounded notion that the church was a suitable place for a lad who was fit for nothing else. Robert Leighton writes reprovingly of men who are 'making it the refuge and forlorn resource of their insufficiency for other callings.'[1] In all these cases there was a harmful 'constraint', whether from tradition, family expectations or desperation to make a living. It is not surprising that such men were, at best, half-hearted in their service.

But surely no-one is constrained in this way now? Perhaps not, although well-meaning Christians sometimes run ahead of the Lord in prematurely encouraging gifted young men towards the pastorate. A pressure of expectancy can be created which is hard to disappoint. But in other ways the danger against which Peter warns us is still a very real one.

A minister may lose enthusiasm for his work. Perhaps he is depressed or discouraged, or illness has sapped his vitality. It may be that an unresponsive people and long years of seemingly fruitless preaching have blunted the edge of his commitment. He may have been neglecting his own relationship with God, not spending time feeding his soul with the Word or communing with the Saviour in prayer. Sin, unacknowledged and unforsaken, may have come between him and the Lord and brought him into a spiritual desert. Whatever the reason, he has little joy in what he is doing.

But he still carries on with his appointed duties. No-one could reasonably accuse him of laziness or neglect. He is punctilious in preaching, visiting and administering. He is like the elder son in the parable of the prodigal, who 'answered and said to his father, Lo, these many years I have been serving you; I never transgressed your commandment at any time' (*Luke* 15:29). A

[1] *Commentary on 1 Peter*, p. 470.

model son? Outwardly yes, but the cold resentment which oozes from every word must have chilled his father to the bone. The pastor may not feel resentful. But something has gone. There is no spring in his step, no sparkle in his eye, no leaping of the heart as he begins each day. He works because he must. The people expect it, he has promised to do it, it is what he is paid for. It is 'by constraint'.

But, says Peter, this is not good enough. The God who looks on the heart is not satisfied with a forced, external obedience. Our work, if it is to please him, must be done 'willingly', with our joyful consent. Paul makes a similar emphasis when writing to the Corinthians about Christian giving: 'Let each one give as he purposes in his heart, not grudgingly or of necessity; for God loves a cheerful giver' (*2 Cor.* 9:7). We may presume that the same God is equally pleased with a cheerful pastor!

We need to pray for a willing spirit. We should ask the Lord to keep us enthusiastic in all our pastoral work. Especially is this important in areas of responsibility which we do not naturally enjoy. Routine administration and all-too-frequent committee meetings can be time-consuming and tedious. Visits must be made to people who ruffle our composure and drain us of energy. Tracing the usage of a verb through a Hebrew lexicon is not everyone's idea of fun. But in all of this, as well as in those parts of our work which are more congenial, we are to serve the Lord with gladness.

A phrase, missing from some translations but occurring in the better manuscripts, shows us the secret: 'not by constraint, but willingly, according to God'. We are working in God's presence, at all times under his gaze. Our Master is enabling us moment by moment. We are seeking in all things his greater glory. Who would not work willingly in such an atmosphere? Even the most unexciting work is transformed when done 'according to God'. As George Herbert wrote:

> *All may of Thee partake;*
> *Nothing can be so mean,*
> *Which with this tincture, 'for Thy sake',*
> *Will not grow bright and clean.*
> *A servant with this clause*
> *Makes drudgery divine.*

ii. 'Not for dishonest gain but eagerly.'

Some ministers reading these words and reflecting on their current salary may be tempted to give way to hollow laughter. 'Gain' of any kind seems a distant prospect. Here, they may think, is one temptation to which they cannot possibly be prone. Even if they wanted to, they could not commit this sin.

Now Peter is not excusing the failure of congregations to provide adequately for their pastors. In no way is he giving leave to the people of God to abandon men and their families to enforced poverty. He agrees with Paul that 'the Lord has commanded that those who preach the gospel should live from the gospel' (*1 Cor.* 9:14). But his focus here is on the pastor himself. Human nature does not change and the love of money can all too easily insinuate itself into our thinking and entwine its tentacles around our hearts.

Evangelicalism is in danger of selling its soul to Mammon. The materialistic spirit is at its most blatant in America, but the rest of the world is rapidly catching up. Religious empires are built up around a single leader or one specialist aspect of ministry. Lacking a proper church base, they require substantial and repeated infusions of cash if they are to keep going. This demand has turned Christian fund-raising into a sophisticated industry whose methods are manipulative and frequently less than honest.

Noted preachers have lavish life-styles and command exorbitant fees for their services. Religious magazines contain more pages of advertisements than of text. They are, it seems, more committed to selling to their readers than to teaching or informing them. Publishers' catalogues have new books every month and new Bible versions almost every year which 'no believer can afford to be without'. Why? Are the publishers concerned for our spiritual wellbeing? They appear to be more interested in making money out of us. Profit is the bottom line.

The commercialism of the world is infecting the church and it is so pervasive that many believers simply do not realise how profoundly they are being influenced. The pastor can be damaged by this pollution and come to see his ministry as little more than a source of revenue.

Temptation is fuelled by the careless way in which church

funds are sometimes handled. Christians tend to be generous and unsuspecting. They will readily entrust money to someone they respect, depending on him to see that it reaches the proper destination. A man who is greedy or needy may find this an opportunity too inviting to resist.

Even apart from these obvious abuses, it is frighteningly easy to become materialistic. When ministers rarely talk together about the things of God, yet grow animated while discussing their expense allowances or pension arrangements, something is sadly wrong. Others seem to know far too much about stocks and shares or where to obtain the best return for investments. Young men entering their first pastorate are being encouraged to conduct detailed negotiations about what is now called 'the package'—their salary, housing and benefits. These things have their place, of course, and no-one would want pastors to be improvident or foolishly unworldly. But is it idealistic or old-fashioned to feel a certain distaste at a man of God who is quite so *au fait* with finance? Is he truly imitating our Lord, who 'though he was rich, yet for your sakes he became poor' and who told us not to 'lay up for yourselves treasures on earth' (*2 Cor.* 8:9; *Matt.* 6:19)?

Nor is it only those with money to whom this warning applies, for a poor man can be just as mercenary as a rich one. Someone on a small income may complain constantly or comment sourly on the possessions of others. His half-joking references to poverty are not as light-hearted as they appear. He is as obsessed with the money he does not have, as other men are with that which they have accumulated. 'If a man fall into it,' writes Leighton, 'he may drown in a small brook, being under water, as well as in the great ocean.'[1]

The 'dishonest gain' may not even be financial at all. It is quite possible to engage in Christian service for prestige or power instead of for the Lord. The principle is exactly the same. Here too the person is motivated by something base or shameful, as the root meaning of the word translated 'dishonest' implies. There is 'something in it' for him.

By contrast, the true pastor is to work 'eagerly', with enthusiasm and passion. He will be wholeheartedly involved

---

[1] Ibid., p. 471.

in what he is doing. He will love the work for its own sake and give himself to it without reserve. Any thought of profit will be the last thing in his mind. Paul used the same word when he told the Romans, 'I am ready (eager) to preach the gospel to you who are in Rome' (*Rom.* 1:15). Was the apostle eager because he had counted up how much he might earn in preaching fees? Never! What filled his soul with joy was the prospect of preaching the free grace of God in Jesus Christ. What was the rubbish of money in comparison?

It is easy to sentimentalise the past, but is it not true that Christians of thirty or forty years ago were less addicted to material things than their descendants today? I am thinking of elderly ministers whom I knew as a boy. There was a disinterestedness in them which is now in danger of being lost. They had not been as well trained as modern pastors. Their libraries were small, with few of the riches available now. In some cases they were not as intelligently aware of Reformed doctrine as they might have been. But one of their virtues was a lack of concern about money. Their knowledge of finance was minimal and their interest in it less. It was obvious to all who knew them that they lived for another world. We could well learn from them.

An earlier example of freedom from the love of money is John Brown of Haddington. Some of his books, notably his *Dictionary of the Bible* and *Self-Interpreting Bible*, passed through many editions, but he received and was content with little financial recompense from them. Shortly before Brown's death in 1787 a friend advised him to arrange for his family to profit from future editions. His reply was emphatic:

No, no; I would not wish that ever there should be the least appearance of the world in me. I can trust my family to Providence; and if, when I am in heaven, it appear that there was one converted by means of anything I ever wrote, I will mark down a hundred pounds; if there should be two, I will say there are two hundred pounds; and, if twenty, there is something of more value than two thousand pounds. That is the reward which I wish.[1]

---

[1] Robert Mackenzie, *John Brown of Haddington* (Banner of Truth Trust, 1964), p. 275.

Such a man had his heart and his treasure in heaven. Little wonder that the last earthly words he spoke were 'My Christ'.

One of the most moving instances of pastoral integrity in this area is found in Samuel's farewell speech to Israel at Saul's coronation. 'Old and gray-headed', he is laying down his charge. But before he does so he addresses the people:

Here I am. Witness against me before the LORD and before his anointed. Whose ox have I taken, or whose donkey . . . or whom have I defrauded? Whom have I oppressed, or from whose hand have I received any bribe with which to blind my eyes? I will restore it to you. And they said, You have not defrauded us or oppressed us, nor have you taken anything from any man's hand. Then he said to them, The LORD is witness against you, and his anointed is witness this day, that you have not found anything in my hand. And they answered, he is witness (*1 Sam.* 12:2–5).

What a testimony! Every pastor should so keep watch over his motivation that he can end his course with his hands clean and his heart unstained by covetousness.

iii. 'Nor as being lords over those entrusted to you, but being examples to the flock.'
Christians are told to 'obey those who rule over you, and be submissive' (*Heb.* 13:17), which implies that the pastor is in a position of considerable authority. He is sometimes better educated than many of his people and he should have a more extensive knowledge of the Bible and understanding of theology than most of them. Living at a time when the ministry is undervalued and when the simpering, bleating vicar is a stock figure of comedy, it is understandable that he will want to magnify his office, stressing its dignity and importance. But herein lies danger.

A good man may, gradually and subconsciously, overreact and forget that he is a servant, not a master. Peter speaks of those who behave 'as being lords'. The verb is used in secular writing of subduing a city—overwhelming all opposition, repressing dissent, conquering and controlling a rebellious people. But to attempt this in the church is blasphemy, a usurping of God's authority. There is only one Lord and the people we serve belong to him and are merely 'entrusted' to us to care for on his behalf.

What are the ways in which men manifest an arrogant, lordly spirit? Some dominate their churches through sheer force of personality or fluency of speech. Their people are not ruled by the gracious leading of the Spirit or by convictions based solidly on truth. They are cowed, rather, by the knowledge, painfully learned, that the pastor will always be able to out-talk or browbeat those who may stand against him. Other leaders cultivate a remote, pompous, authoritarian manner—what John Calvin calls an 'imperious strictness'. They are dismissive or sarcastic when approached, with little in their personality to attract confidence or even an honest expression of opinion.

Some men insist on having their own way in every detail of church life, even the most minute. Nothing can happen unless it has been pastorally approved. Whether it be the colour of curtains for the church hall or the menu for the congregational lunch, it seems that there is no-one else within the fellowship with ability, gifts or common sense. All must be deferred to the ecclesiastical tyrant, who has taken his motto from Shakespeare: 'I am Sir Oracle, And when I ope my lips, let no dog bark!'. This is 'lording'.

Whenever a group of leaders goes beyond Scripture and starts imposing regulations and edicts which have no biblical warrant, clear or implied, God's lordship is being denied. When overseers display an unwarranted intrusiveness into their people's lives, probing into private details which are none of their concern, they are forgetting their place. Pastors who bully the young or vulnerable are cowboys, not shepherds. To ostracise someone who has dared to disagree, however conscientiously, is a disgraceful abuse of power.

Even the modern mania for counselling can threaten the liberty of God's children. In some evangelical circles, the spiritual therapist is taking over from the Roman priest as father or mother confessor. Everyone, it seems, needs a 'guru' in whom to confide and from whom to receive direction. This can all too easily blur the wonder and immediacy of our relationship with our only Lord. Each of us has personal and immediate access to our heavenly Father, in whom are all the resources we can ever need.

The temptation to act as a 'lord' is a real one. The churches are in chaos and confusion. Individualism is running rampant, as in the period when 'there was no king in Israel; everyone did what was right in his own eyes' (*Judges* 21:25). The need for strong, directive Christian leadership was seldom more urgent than it is today.

But not 'lordship'. Christ's words are categorical: 'You know that the rulers of the Gentiles lord it over them, and those who are great exercise authority over them. Yet it shall not be so among you' (*Matt.* 20:25,26).

Instead, we are to be 'examples to the flock'. Here is the key factor in pastoral work. We are to follow Christ in such a way that those for whom we care may safely follow us. Our lives are to enforce what our lips profess. For a pastor to practise what he preaches means more than rehearsing his sermon. He is to be a living, acting illustration of the gospel.

It has often been noted that the qualities required of an elder (for example in 1 Timothy 3 or Titus 1) are essentially the same as those expected from all believers. This is because the elder is to represent to the people the character of the mature Christian, not the unattainable talents of the specialist. He is to be, to a great extent, what they should all aspire to become. He is their 'example'.

We simply cannot overestimate the immense power of such lives. Godly men exert a powerful and lasting influence in a church. Their demeanour is a benediction. Their very presence can calm the angry or give new heart to the discouraged. They may not say or do anything remarkable. Their abilities may be limited. But a fragrance of Christ accompanies them. To be with them is to be blessed. Such men will be respected and remembered when the would-be dictators are thankfully forgotten.

Every under-shepherd of God's flock must choose between alternatives which are mutually exclusive—to domineer or to set an example. The elder who domineers can set no example for any Christian to follow. The exemplary elder, on the other hand, will never be domineering. One or the other—which am I?

16

The pastor's reward

'And when the Chief Shepherd appears, you will receive the crown of glory that does not fade away.'

One of the notable elements in Peter's letters is the way in which he frequently points his readers forward to the life to come. His mind is full of the return of Christ, the day of judgment and the glory of heaven and this perspective influences his writing profoundly. He is a pastor who lives and teaches always in the light of eternity.

This emphasis is strikingly evident in the opening verses of his first epistle. After initial greetings he moves instantly and repeatedly to the last things: '. . . an inheritance incorruptible and undefiled . . . reserved in heaven for you . . . salvation ready to be revealed in the last time . . . that the genuineness of your faith . . . may be found to praise, honour and glory at the revelation of Jesus Christ' (*1 Pet.* 1:4,5,7). He begins the next section on the same note: 'Therefore gird up the loins of your mind, be sober, and rest your hope fully upon the grace that is to be brought to you at the revelation of Jesus Christ' (1:13). When dealing with practical duties, the motivation offered is identical: 'But the end of all things is at hand; therefore be serious and watchful in your prayers' (4:7). The same theme is continued in the second letter, when he urges his readers to fruitful growth in the faith with the reminder that 'so an entrance will be supplied to you abundantly into the everlasting kingdom of our Lord and Saviour Jesus Christ' (*2 Pet.* 1:11). The last words from the apostle's pen, chapter three of 2 Peter, form one of the most thorough treatments of the second coming of Christ in the New Testament.

Why is he so interested in the future? Why does this pastor

direct the eyes of his flock with such persistence to the last things? Is he a 'prophecy addict', obsessed with the details of millennial interpretation or apocalyptic symbolism? Not at all. Peter emphasises the return of Jesus and what will follow because these realities are overwhelmingly precious to him and because they are of the greatest possible practical value to his readers. His purpose is pastoral throughout.

How can people be stirred up to flee sin and pursue holiness? By directing their attention to the day of judgment. How can they be guided in making daily decisions and setting earthly priorities? By teaching them to look at everything from that heavenly perspective which alone is ultimately significant. How can he enable those who are grief-stricken, suffering and discouraged to endure and even to rejoice? By reminding them of the unfading inheritance which is waiting for them in glory. Peter wants to make Christians more heavenly-minded. Nothing will help them more than this.

If ordinary believers are to be heavenly-minded, then surely those who lead them should be even more so. But this is an emphasis which seems to be missing from modern pastoral consciousness. Ministers are so concerned with being seen to be relevant to society around them, so anxious to avoid any charge of being escapist or other-worldly that they bend over backwards to establish their this-worldly credentials. They would like to be seen as experts in healing the present hurt, scratching the current itch, meeting the crying need. They want to major in the here-and-now.

In some respects, of course, that is a good thing. Part of the wonder of the gospel is that Christ saves us here and now, not just in the invisible future. He meets us where we are and enables us to cope with reality as it is at present. He is with us at this moment by his Spirit, involved in all the details of our daily existence. Pastors are to reflect that practical interest as they move among their people. Yet, in our concern for present usefulness, we can easily forget what is most valuable of all.

One phrase had burnt itself into my mind as I began my ministry in 1968. It was the old unbelieving sneer that Christians were 'too heavenly-minded to be of any earthly use' and I was determined to disprove it. Authors such as Francis Schaeffer had taught me that the Bible had something to say about every sphere of human life. It thrilled me to realise that scriptural principles were relevant for the politician, the businessman and the artist and could be applied to economics and to science as well as to religion. If God's Word were believed and obeyed, life on earth would be transformed. I still believe these truths today. As I look back however, my early ministry was unbalanced in this direction. I was spiritually and pastorally short-sighted. I may not have paid too much attention to the things of time, but I certainly gave too little thought to the realities of eternity.

This is a particular temptation for us when we are young and healthy, when life is sweet and sadness a stranger. It is also characteristic of modern Western societies which are prosperous and relatively peaceful. We are comfortable where we are, with everything around us to cater for our felt needs. This world is compellingly pleasant and we feel little interest in any other. In such an atmosphere, our spiritual focus is earth-bound and immediate.

But both the Bible and history are against us. Past Christian generations, less pampered and secure, lived far more consistently in the light of eternity. They understood the fragility and imperfection of this life better than we do and were correspondingly more enthralled with the joys of the life to come. Poor and persecuted, it was no great wrench for them to confess 'that they were strangers and pilgrims on the earth' (*Heb.* 11:13). We need to relearn this perspective. Because, contrary to what unbelievers claim, those who are of most earthly use are precisely those who are most heavenly-minded.

That is why Peter, as he comes to the end of his exhortation to the elders, urges them to look forward to the return of Christ. Like their people, they too are to be other-worldly in this sense. An awareness of what will happen in the future is to motivate their present pastoral ministry. Everything is be done in the light of what they will experience 'when the Chief Shepherd appears'.

The expression 'Chief Shepherd' is found only here in the

New Testament, although Hebrews 13:20 comes close with 'our Lord Jesus, that great Shepherd of the sheep'. It could be intimidating for under-shepherds to be reminded of the One under whose authority they are and to whom they are responsible. But Peter uses it here as a stimulus and encouragement. As 'fellow-elder' brought the apostle close to those to whom he was writing, so 'Chief Shepherd' points to Christ's intimate connection with every pastor.

Because there is a chief shepherd, we have an example to follow in our work. We do not have to muddle through on our own, trying to guess how our duties should be carried out. We have a mentor to whom we can go for guidance. He is the pattern, the template for all faithful ministry. If we model ourselves on him and try to please him in all we do, we cannot go far wrong.

His nearness also lifts from us the crushing weight of ultimate responsibility. The well-being of the flock does not finally depend on us. It is in the hands of the One who died for the sheep, to whom alone they belong. Christ, the chief shepherd, cares for them more than we do. He is more involved in their oversight than we are. He is able to compensate for our shortcomings and failures and to keep his sheep and bring them safely to glory. We can give our all to the pastorate, relaxed in the knowledge that wiser, stronger hands are directing our imperfect efforts and overruling our many blunders. What an encouragement when a bewildered apprentice can look round and see, close by, the supremely competent Master!

For the chief shepherd is with us now, though we cannot see him. Yet the day is approaching when he will 'appear' in glory. He will come on the clouds of heaven with the voice of an archangel and every eye will see him. This final manifestation of Christ will have several purposes. But the one outlined here is to reward his faithful pastors: 'And when the Chief Shepherd appears, you will receive the crown of glory that does not fade away.'

The crown was the gold medal of the ancient world, awarded to the winner in a race or the victor in a battle. It was a coveted mark of high achievement and unusual honour, granted only to the very few. In Christ's kingdom, the under-shepherds are among those who will qualify for that prize. But it will be a crown of a very different kind from that awarded at the Greek Olympics.

'You will receive the crown of glory that does not fade away'. The crown given to the athlete or warrior was woven from leaves of olive or myrtle, or strands of wild parsley. For a few hours it would encircle the winner's head. But soon it would dry out and wither, to be thrown aside and forgotten. The crown of glory, on the other hand, will never fade, but remain fresh and new to all eternity.

What is this crown? It is glory itself, everlasting life, the permanent possession of a share in the blessedness of heaven. Just as 'the crown of life' (*James* 1:12; *Rev.* 2:10) is the crown which is life, so 'the crown of glory' is the crown which is composed of glory. That glory is unfading and everlasting. It is the glory of the Lord himself, who will be 'a crown of glory and a diadem of beauty' (*Isa.* 28:5) to his people.

The crown is also a mark of undying honour and we can see, even in this life, how it is awarded. The great men and women of the earth strut their hour upon the world stage, in all their pride and pomp. They dominate the media and their names and doings are on the lips of all. Then they fall from power or die and how quickly they are forgotten! Who now remembers the politician, film-star or military leader of thirty years ago? Who thinks of them or gives thanks for them? No-one. But I have sat with men and women in their seventies and listened as they spoke of a minister of their childhood, dead for half a century or more. That man made no headlines and was never listed in *Who's Who*. Yet his people still remember him with gratitude. Their faces soften and their eyes light up as they recall his preaching and his counsel. They tell their children and grand-children of what he meant to them and to others. Every faithful pastor can expect such a memorial. He will live in many hearts long after he has passed away. The impact of his life and ministry will continue down through the generations. 'The righteous will be in everlasting remembrance' (*Psa.* 112:6).

To say 'everlasting remembrance' is no exaggeration, because our relationship with our people will continue into heaven. How shall we feel when we see in glory those who were entrusted to our care on earth? How shall we feel when we meet those who were brought to faith through our preaching, guided safely by our counsel, matured and strengthened by our care? Will we not experience an exultant, humble gladness when we realise that, in spite of much failure and felt weakness, we have been enabled to play a part in their everlasting happiness? When they speak freely of what God did for them through us, will our hearts not be filled to overflowing?

Samuel Rutherford, the Covenanting preacher, was imprisoned in Aberdeen for loyalty to King Jesus. From that prison, on 13 July, 1637, he appealed affectionately to his congregation to trust the Saviour: 'My witness is above; your heaven would be two heavens to me, and the salvation of you all as two salvations to me'. The pastor, meeting even one soul from his flock at God's right hand, will have 'two heavens, two salvations'. We may hope to meet many more of our people than that. There will, no doubt, be surprises. Some will rendezvous with us whom we never expected to see. Is that not an unfading crown of glory? Well could Paul describe his congregation in Philippi as 'my beloved and longed-for brethren, my joy and crown' (*Phil.* 4:1).

Best of all will be the look on our Saviour's face as we come to stand before him. The under-shepherds will render their account to the chief shepherd. When Jacob reported to Laban, it was with a mixture of pride in work well done and self-pity at the cost of his labours: 'These twenty years I have been with you; your ewes have not miscarried their young, and I have not eaten the rams of your flock. There I was! In the day the drought consumed me, and the frost by night, and my sleep departed from my eyes' (*Gen.* 31:38,40). When we report to our master, we will give him all the glory for anything we have accomplished. We will certainly not regret, or even refer to, the labour we undertook or the suffering we experienced. We will not feel that we have wasted our lives. We will wish only that we could have done far more.

The Chief Shepherd will look at us with love and pleasure. He will regard with special honour those pastors whose charges were unusually difficult—the sheep wayward, the pasture barren and the wolves numerous. But all his servants will share in his approval. We will gaze into his face and hear his voice: 'Well done, good and faithful servant; you were faithful over a few things, I will make you ruler over many things. Enter into the joy of your Lord' (*Matt.* 25:21). That will be a crown of glory indeed!

Robert Leighton, as he meditates on it, rises to heights of holy eloquence:

A crown of glory, pure, unmixed glory, without any ingrediency of pride or sinful vanity, or any danger of it . . . May they not well trample on base gain and vain applause, who have this crown to look to? . . . All labour is sweet for it. And what is there here to be desired to detain our hearts, that we should not most willingly let go, to rest from our labours, and receive our crown? Was ever any king sad to think that the day of his coronation drew nigh? And then, there will be no envy, nor jealousies; all will be kings, each with his own crown, each rejoicing in the glory of the others, and all in HIS, who that day shall be All in All.[1]

Here is our motivation, our true reward. Pastors enjoy many compensations here and now. Our work itself is a privilege. We rejoice when we see a measure of blessing on our labours and exclaim with Paul: 'Now thanks be to God who always leads us in triumph in Christ, and through us diffuses the fragrance of his knowledge in every place' (*2 Cor.* 2:14). Even when apparent success is lacking, we experience inner peace in knowing that we are in the place of God's appointing and that he appreciates our efforts. The Servant of the Lord who says, 'I have laboured in vain, I have spent my strength for nothing and in vain', immediately continues: 'Yet surely my just reward is with the LORD, And my work with my God' (*Isa.* 49:4). But the chief orientation of our service and our living is always a future one. In the words of John Calvin[2]:

Unless pastors keep this end in view, it can never come about that they will proceed in the course of their calling in earnest . . . because there are innumerable hindrances which can discourage the most prudent. They have often to do with ungrateful men, from whom

---

[1] *Commentary on 1 Peter*, pp. 472–3.
[2] John Calvin, *Hebrews and 1 & 2 Peter* (Saint Andrew Press, 1963), p. 317

they receive an unworthy reward; long and great labours are often in vain; Satan sometimes prevails with his wicked devices. So then, to prevent the faithful servant of Christ from being cast down, there is this one and only remedy, to turn his eyes to the coming of Christ.

Let us give thanks for the responsibility which is ours. Let us seek the Master's forgiveness for our failures and return to our work with new devotion. 'When the Chief Shepherd appears, you will receive the crown of glory that does not fade away.' What greater encouragement do we need?

Epilogue

Simon Peter, a servant and apostle of Jesus Christ, To those who have obtained like precious faith with us by the righteousness of our God and Saviour Jesus Christ: Grace and peace be multiplied to you in the knowledge of God and of Jesus our Lord, as His divine power has given to us all things that pertain to life and godliness, through the knowledge of Him who called us by glory and virtue, by which have been given to us exceedingly great and precious promises, that through these you may be partakers of the divine nature . . . Therefore, brethren, be even more diligent to make your calling and election sure, for if you do these things you will never stumble; for so an entrance will be supplied to you abundantly into the everlasting kingdom of our Lord and Saviour Jesus Christ. Therefore I will not be negligent to remind you always of these things, though you know them and are established in the present truth. Yes, I think it is right, as long as I am in this tent, to stir you up by reminding you, knowing that shortly I must put off my tent, just as our Lord Jesus Christ showed me. Moreover I will be careful to ensure that you always have a reminder of these things after my decease . . . Therefore, beloved, looking forward to these things, be diligent to be found by Him in peace, without spot and blameless . . . Since you know these things beforehand, beware lest you also fall from your own steadfastness, being led away with the error of the wicked; but grow in the grace and knowledge of our Lord and Saviour Jesus Christ. To Him be the glory both now and forever. Amen

(*2 Pet.* 1:1–4, 10–15; 3:14, 17–18)

[140]

Appendix

Are Peter's own words recorded in his sermons?

Until comparatively recently this would have seemed an unnecessary question with an obvious answer. But modern attacks on the historical reliability of Scripture have extended to the speeches in Acts and it is now commonly suggested that what we have in these sermons is Luke's version of what Peter might have said, not the *ipsissima verba* of the apostle.

Eduard Schweizer summed up the situation in 1957 when he wrote that 'it has been more and more widely recognized that the speeches are basically compositions by the author of Acts who, to be sure, utilized different kinds of material for particular passages'.[1] I. Howard Marshall, although arguing for the substantial historicity of the speeches, asserts that 'there are a number of points which indicate that the speeches were never meant to be verbatim reports'. His conclusion is 'that Luke could and did compose appropriate remarks for his speakers, and that we do him an injustice if we expect from him verbatim accounts of each and every speech'.[2]

The subject of the speeches in Acts has attracted an immense amount of scholarly literature and is too complex to be considered in this brief appendix. The speeches of Paul, for example, are a field of study in themselves. What is presented here is no more than a modest defence of the proposition that in the records of Peter's sermons we have an accurate report of what he did in fact say.

[1] F. F. Bruce, *The Acts of the Apostles*, 3rd edition (Leicester: Apollos, 1990), pp. 36–7.
[2] I. Howard Marshall, *The Acts of the Apostles* (Leicester: IVP, 1980), pp. 41–2.

Why is there doubt?

Critics have questioned the accuracy of these speeches on various grounds. The nineteenth-century Tübingen school dismissed the entire Book of Acts as an anonymous second century attempt to cover over a supposed conflict between Peter and Paul. Elements of this subsequently discredited view resurfaced in Ernst Haenchen's massive commentary, published in English in 1971. In this work, according to Marshall, 'the narrative was claimed to have little basis in tradition, to be full of historical inconsistencies and improbabilities, and to be basically the product of the fertile mind of a historical novelist with little or no concern for such tiresome things as facts'.[1]

Other scholars, while more positive about the reliability of the book as a whole, have had difficulty in accepting the speeches as verbatim accounts. One obstacle has been the claim that ancient historians were not concerned with verbal precision, but aimed rather at creating speeches which would be appropriate for the occasion and the speaker. The writing of history was seen as a literary and rhetorical enterprise, to be judged quite as much by the creative skill employed as by the accuracy of the reporting. The Roman orator, Cicero, disparaged those who 'did not embellish their facts, but were chroniclers and nothing more'.[2] Thucydides, the greatest of the Greek historians, gives a classic explanation of his methodology at the beginning of his History of the Peloponnesian War:

With reference to the speeches in this history, some were delivered before the war began, others while it was going on; some I heard myself, others I got from various quarters; it was in all cases difficult to carry them word for word in one's memory, so my habit has been to make the speakers say what was in my opinion demanded of them by the various occasions, of course adhering as closely as possible to the general sense of what they really said.[3]

[1] Ibid., p. 35.
[2] Conrad Gempf, *Public Speaking and Published Accounts* in *The Book of Acts in its First Century Setting*, vol. 1, B. W. Winter and A. D. Clarke, eds. (Carlisle: Paternoster Press, 1993), p. 277.
[3] *History of the Peloponnesian War*, 1:22, cited in *The Portable Greek Historians*, M. I. Finley, ed. (New York: Penguin Books, 1980), pp. 230–1.

In this context, it is claimed that we cannot expect from Luke a stenographic accuracy which would have been unique in his time.

A more nuanced view is that, in the ancient world, the point of rhetoric was to recreate an event rather than just convey a series of words. The orator was a figure of power, comparable to the general of an army. His speeches were designed to produce results by moving his audience and the impact of what he said was far more important than the precise vocabulary which he used. This holds good for literature and so:

Just as a writer was expected to represent faithfully the strategies, tactics and results of a battle, but not necessarily all the fine movements of each combatant, so a writer was expected to represent faithfully the strategies, tactics and results of a speech, without necessarily recording the exact words used on the day.[1]

As applied to Luke and the speeches he records, this would mean that the quest for verbal accuracy is misconceived. His account, in this view, would be reliable even if he put his own words into Peter's mouth. What is important is that he describes the event correctly—the general sense of what was said and the resulting impact upon the hearers. Conrad Gempf suggests that:

whatever our view of their historical worth, we must stop approaching the speeches in Acts with a 20th century preconception and learn instead to view them in the setting of first-century conventions.. We must learn to think of the public speeches not as (accurate or falsified) transcript/summaries of the words of famous people, but rather as records (faithful or unfaithful) of historical events.[2]

Other objections are of a more practical nature. How could Luke possibly remember speeches word for word? How could he record what was said on occasions where he was not present? Martin Dibelius, one of the early twentieth century critics of the speeches, describes them as 'inventions of the author. For they are too short to have been actually given in this form; they are too similar to one another to have

[1] Gempf, op. cit., p. 264.
[2] Ibid., pp. 302–3.

come from different persons; and in their content they occasionally reproduce a later standpoint (e.g. what Peter and James say about the law in chap.xv)'.[1]

In face of this weight of negative critical opinion, readers of Scripture may be tempted to capitulate and accept the speeches as deriving more from Luke than from Peter.

Does it really matter?

We readily admit that Luke is providing us, on each occasion, with no more than a brief summary of what Peter said. The sermon on the day of Pentecost, the longest of the four we considered, takes approximately five minutes to read aloud. We may presume that Peter preached for a much longer period of time. What we have is an outline of the message, as Luke himself indicates (2:40).

It is also possible that he paraphrased to a small extent, as he transferred Peter's Aramaic to Greek. This could explain the stylistic similarities which some have claimed to find between the speeches of Peter and Paul.

It might even be thought feasible to maintain the inspiration of Scripture while holding to Lukan creativity in recording the speeches. After all, the New Testament writers do not always quote precisely from the Old Testament. We accept the changes they introduced as having been made under the guidance of the Spirit and therefore as being fully the Word of God. Why then can we not receive Luke's record as the inspired account of Peter's preaching, without worrying about whether or not it gives us the very words of the speaker? Surely, if the words we have are those God intended for us, that is all that matters?

But such an approach, initially attractive, is fraught with danger. Once we accept that words which are claimed to have been spoken by Peter were in fact created years later by some-one else, we have started down a slippery slope to disaster. Would the same apply to the words of our Lord? That is exactly what form and redaction critics would have us believe. For most of this century they have been chipping away at the Gospels until, in their opinion, there is little left which goes back to the time of Christ. The link with history has been snapped and instead of

[1] Bruce, op. cit., p. 36.

[144]

the words and actions of Jesus we have only what the later church believed and taught about him—a pathetic substitute!

Critics of the speeches are inviting us, gently and plausibly, down the same path. We must refuse the invitation. There is no reason to doubt that we have, in the Pentecost sermon for example, the very words of Peter. Difficulties are negligible, the evidence in favour considerable. We examine it first in general, then in more specific terms.

General evidence

1. The nature of Scripture

At the root of much modern criticism of Scripture is a failure, deliberate or unconscious, to acknowledge its uniqueness. As the inspired Word of God, it is in a category completely its own. A discussion of the nature of inspiration is outside the scope of this appendix, but it must be asserted that the Bible can never be limited or judged by comparison with other literature. What uninspired writers of the time may or may not have done can never be determinative. We are in no position to decide what may or may not have been possible for Luke when recording these speeches. The difficulties of accurately recording spoken words have been exaggerated. Quintilian, for example, who wrote on rhetoric in the first century A.D., mentions the practice of taking short-hand notes of orations.[1] The human memory was a very much more powerful instrument in the first century than in the information-saturated twentieth.[2]

In the final analysis, however, what is important is that Luke was one of the 'holy men of God' who 'spoke as they were moved by the Holy Spirit' (*2 Pet.* 1:21). He inherited the promise of Jesus that 'the Helper, the Holy Spirit, whom the Father will send in my name . . . will teach you all things, and bring to your remembrance all things that I said to you' (*John* 14:26). As B. B. Warfield comments on 'given by inspiration of God' (*theopneustos*) in 2 Timothy 3:16: 'What it says of Scripture is . . . that it is . . .the product of the creative

---

[1] Gempf, op. cit., p. 299.
[2] See, for example, the brief discussion of the work of Riesenfeld, Gerhardsson and others in Donald Guthrie, *New Testament Introduction*, 4th ed. (Leicester: Apollos, 1990), pp. 1031–5.

breath of God . . . Paul . . . asserts with as much energy as he could employ that Scripture is the product of a specifically Divine operation'.[1]

2. Luke the historian

In spite of persistent questioning, especially by German scholars, of Luke's reliability, it is now generally admitted that he is an exceptionally careful and accurate historian. He moves, without stumbling, through the notorious intricacies of official titles: 'proconsuls' in senatorial provinces like Cyprus (*Acts* 13:7); 'praetors' in Philippi (16:20); 'politarchs' in Thessalonica (17:6) and 'Asiarchs' in Ephesus (19:31). His geographical locations are precise: 'Perga in Pamphylia' (13:13); 'Philippi, which is the foremost city of that part of Macedonia, a colony' (16:12); 'Fair Havens, near the city of Lasea' (27:8); 'Phoenix, a harbour of Crete opening toward the southwest and northwest' (27:12).

Luke's detailed knowledge has been confirmed by A. N. Sherwin-White, a professional classical historian:

For Acts the confirmation of historicity is overwhelming. Any attempt to reject its basic historicity even in matters of detail must now appear absurd. Roman historians have long taken it for granted.[2]

Referring to the legal accuracy of the accounts of Paul's court appearances, he writes:

As documents these narratives belong to the same historical series as the record of provincial and imperial trials in epigraphical and literary sources of the first and early second centuries A.D.[3]

It would be surprising if such a precise writer were to put his own words into the mouths of his main characters. F. J. Foakes-Jackson, writing in 1931, was willing to accept that Luke had modified the speeches to some extent. Yet he recognised their quality:

[1] B. B. Warfield, *The Inspiration and Authority of the Bible* (Nutley: Presbyterian and Reformed, 1970), p. 133.
[2] A. N. Sherwin-White, *Roman Society and Roman Law in the New Testament* (Oxford University Press, 1963), pp. 120–1, 186.
[3] Ibid.

Whatever these speeches may be, it cannot be disputed that they are wonderfully varied as to their character, and as a rule admirably suited to the occasion on which they were delivered. Luke seems to have been able to give us an extraordinarily accurate picture of the undeveloped theology of the earliest Christians, and to enable us to determine the character of the most primitive presentation of the gospel. However produced, the speeches in Acts are masterpieces, and deserve the most careful attention.[1]

In his Gospel, Luke is at pains to record accurately the words of Christ. F. F. Bruce recognises this:

It is agreed by Synoptic students that Luke reports with great faithfulness the sayings and speeches which he found in his Gospel sources . . . If this is the verdict on Luke in places where his fidelity to his source can be controlled, we should not without good reason suppose that he was not equally faithful where his sources are no longer available for comparison.[2]

Surprisingly, however, he later denies the relevance of this for the apostolic speeches on the grounds that:

there was this difference in Acts: in Luke the sayings and speeches were utterances of the Lord and therefore vested with special sanctity, so that they might not be materially altered; Peter, Paul, and the other early Christians whose words are reported in Acts were not on a level with him.[3]

I. H. Marshall agrees and says:

while it is very probable that the teaching of Jesus was especially remembered by his disciples, and indeed that they specifically learned some of what he taught them, it is much less likely that audiences remembered what early Christian preachers said.[4]

This surely betrays a defective view of inspiration. It may be the custom for some modern publishers to produce editions

[1] Bruce, op. cit., p. 39.
[2] F. F. Bruce, *The Acts of the Apostles: the Greek Text with Introduction and Commentary* (Grand Rapids: Eerdmans, 1965), pp. 18–9.
[3] *Acts of the Apostles*, 3rd ed. (Leicester: Apollos, 1990), p. 35.
[4] Marshall, op. cit., p. 41.

of the New Testament which have the words of our Lord printed in red type, but such a practice is more sentimental than scriptural. There is no basis for holding that the sayings of Christ were valued more highly than the inspired words of the apostles, or possessed a 'special sanctity' all their own. Peter condemned those who 'twist to their own destruction' the recent writings of his colleague Paul, 'as they do also the rest of the Scriptures' (2 Pet. 3:16). 'All Scripture' (2 Tim. 3:16) is equally inspired and the speeches in both Gospels and Acts were recorded with identical precision.

3. Ancient historiography

Even in the unlikely event of Luke's being influenced to some degree by the canons of the historians, it is an over-simplification to suggest that all ancient writers were expected to be creative in their recording of speeches. Thucydides' statement of method has already been quoted. He acknowledges that his habit was 'to make the speakers say what was in my opinion demanded of them by the various occasions'. But there is almost a note of regret or apology here. It was because he found it 'difficult to carry them word for word in one's memory' and he aimed always at 'adhering as closely as possible to the general sense of what they really said'.

The Greek historian Polybius, who wrote in the second century B.C., and thus nearer the New Testament period than Thucydides, was a trenchant defender of precision. He argued that the historian should:

simply record what really happened and what really was said, however commonplace ... The peculiar function of history is to discover, in the first place, the words actually spoken, whatever they were.[1]

He criticises the historian Timaeus for composing speeches for his own purposes:

I must speak of the principle on which he composes his public speeches . . . Can anyone who reads them help noticing that Timaeus has untruthfully reported them in his work and has done so of set purpose? For he has not set down the words spoken nor the

[1] Gempf, op. cit., p. 271.

sense of what was really said, but having made up his mind as to what ought to have been said, he recounts all these speeches and all else that follows upon events like a man in a school of rhetoric attempting to speak on a given subject, and shows off his oratorical power, but gives no report of what was actually spoken.[1]

This quotation alone proves that some at least in antiquity expected accurate verbal reporting in speeches and that it cannot be maintained that Luke, in using his own words, would have been following a universal and unquestioned convention. Colin Hemer has a more balanced grasp of the evidence when he writes: 'There are two basic things to stress: that ancient historiography is an extremely complicated business and that it is not easy to specify exactly how Luke relates to it.'[2]

Enough has been said to show that the currently fashionable haste to dismiss the possibility of Luke reporting verbatim what was said on each occasion as impossible and anachronistic rests on no solid foundation. It is, rather, the product of critical presuppositions and preferences whose basis is more philosophical than factual.

Specific evidence

When we look in detail at Peter's sermons we find a striking correspondence between them and other parts of the New Testament with which he is associated. These correspondences are by no means conclusive, but they certainly point in the direction of Petrine authorship.

1. Mark and Peter

It has long been recognised that Mark, who was not one of the Twelve, obtained most of the material for his Gospel from Peter. Papias, second century bishop of Hierapolis, claims to quote the apostle John when he writes that 'Mark became Peter's interpreter and wrote accurately all that he remembered, not, indeed, in order, of the things said or done by the Lord. For he had not heard the Lord, nor had he followed him, but later on, as I said, followed Peter, who used to give

---

[1] Ibid., p. 272.
[2] Ibid., p. 298.

the teaching as necessity demanded . . .'[1] In other words, Mark used Peter's preaching as the basis for his Gospel. This assertion has never been seriously questioned and the influence of Peter is clearly pervasive in Mark's writing.

A point of particular interest, however, is the remarkable similarity between the outline of the message preached in the house of Cornelius (*Acts* 10:34–43) and the structure of the second Gospel. In his sermon Peter makes the following basic points:

a) The word 'was proclaimed throughout all Judea and began from Galilee'.
b) 'After the baptism which John preached'.
c) 'How God anointed Jesus of Nazareth with the Holy Spirit and with power'.
d) 'Who went about doing good and healing all who were oppressed by the devil, for God was with Him'.
e) 'And we are witnesses of all things which He did both in the land of the Jews and in Jerusalem'.
f) 'Whom they killed by hanging on a tree'.
g) 'Him God raised up on the third day and showed Him openly'.

This is an almost perfect summary of Mark's Gospel. In the first fourteen verses Mark tells us that 'John came baptizing in the wilderness and preaching . . . And all the land of Judea, and those from Jerusalem, went out to him'; Jesus is then baptized by John in the Jordan, after which the Spirit descends upon him and the voice from heaven identifies him as God's beloved Son. After 'John was put in prison, Jesus came to Galilee, preaching the gospel of the kingdom of God'. From 1:16–10:52 he describes Jesus' mighty ministry in Galilee, characterised by healings and exorcisms, followed by the withdrawal beyond Galilee and journey to Jerusalem. Chapters 11–13 deal with the Jerusalem ministry, while 14 and 15 describe the events which culminated in Christ's crucifixion. Chapter 16 brings the Gospel story to an end with the triumphant cry, 'He is risen!'[2]

---

[1] D. A. Carson, D. J. Moo and L. Morris, *An Introduction to the New Testament* (Grand Rapids: Apollos, 1992), p. 92.
[2] See William L. Lane, *The Gospel of Mark* (Grand Rapids: Eerdmans, 1974), pp. 10–11.

At the very least, we can say that Mark's Gospel is patterned along similar lines to the preaching recorded in Acts 10. If that sermon derives from Peter, his mentor, such similarity is perfectly understandable. If, on the other hand, it is largely the work of Luke, how can we explain the correspondence? Is it a mere coincidence? The evidence points towards a genuine record of what Peter actually said, no doubt an outline which he regularly used in gospel preaching.

2. Acts and 1 Peter

If the sermons in Acts contain Peter's own words, we should expect to find echoes in his epistles. This proves to be the case, for 'there is a remarkable body of common thought between 1 Peter and speeches attributed to Peter in Acts'.[1] The following examples illustrate the presence of similar themes and expressions:

a) The sufferings and glory of Christ are in fulfilment of prophecy (*Acts* 2:16f; 3:18; *1 Pet.* 1:10f).

b) The crucifixion was foreordained by God (*Acts* 2:23 [*prognosei*]; *1 Pet.* 1:20 [*proegnosmenou*]).

c) Christ is appointed as judge of both the living and the dead (*Acts* 10:42; *1 Pet.* 4:5).

d) The 'stone' prophecy from Psalm 118:22, remembered no doubt from the Saviour's words in Matthew 21:42, is applied to Christ, (*Acts* 4:11; *1 Pet.* 2:7).

e) The term *xulon*—'wood, tree', from Deuteronomy 21:22f, is applied to the cross (*Acts* 5:30; 10:39; *1 Pet.* 2:24).

f) The unusual *prosopolemptes*—'partial'—of Acts 10:34 is matched by *aprosopolemptos*—'without partiality'—in 1 Peter 1:17.

g) 'Ignorance' is a characteristic of pre-conversion life (*Acts* 3:17; *1 Pet.* 1:14).

We do not claim that these ideas and words are unique to Peter. Paul, for example, uses *xulon* in Acts 13:29 and Galatians

---

[1] Andrew F. Walls in Alan M. Stibbs, *The First Epistle General of Peter* (London: Tyndale Press, 1962), p. 35.

3:13 and *prosopolempsia* in Romans 2:11, Ephesians 6:7 and Colossians 3:25. But the cumulative force of the similarities is impressive. It strains credulity to claim that Luke could have composed speeches so uncannily close to the language of a letter which he would not have seen at the time when he was writing. E. G. Selwyn's conclusion seems unassailable:

Few would suggest that the parallels of thought and phrase between the speeches and 1 Peter are based upon St Luke's reading of the Epistle . . . On the other hand, they are what might be expected if both alike are utterances of the same mind, given on different occasions. The connexion, that is to say, is not literary but historical: the common ground lies in the mind of St Peter who gave, and was known to have given, teaching along these lines and to a great extent in these terms.[1]

One of Hans Christian Andersen's most famous stories for children is *The Emperor's New Clothes*. It tells of a pair of tricksters who deceived a gullible people into admiring a non-existent set of clothes which, it was claimed, only the wise could see. The fraud was exposed only when an innocent child, too simple to worry about his reputation, shouted out: 'The emperor has nothing on!'.

There is a parallel here with much modern 'scholarship'. Its assertions are sweeping and made with an intimidating display of knowledge. On closer examination, however, they prove flimsy and unsubstantiated. It is time for those with little academic reputation to lose to speak out plainly. Throughout the centuries, ordinary readers of the Bible have believed that 'Then Peter said to them' (*Acts* 4:12) means exactly what it says. They are quite right.

---

[1] E. G. Selwyn, *The First Epistle of St Peter* (London: Macmillan, 1946), p. 36.